Shadow Space

Shadow Space

Suicides and the Predicament of Rural India

A.R. Vasavi

Three Essays
COLLECTIVE

First Edition January 2012

ISBN 978-81-88789-81-8

Three Essays
COLLECTIVE

B-957 Palam Vihar, GURGAON (Haryana) 122 017 India
Phone: 91-124 2369023, +91 98681 26587, +91 98683 44843
info@threeessays.com Website: www.threeessays.com
Printed and bound at Glorious Printers, New Delhi

Contents

INTRODUCTION

LOCATING THE SUICIDES

> Between 1997 and 2006 an average of seventeen thousand, three hundred and sixty six agriculturists committed suicide every year in India. By the end of 2008, one lakh, ninety nine thousand, one hundred and thirty-two agriculturists had committed suicide.
>
> **National Crime Records Bureau, Government of India, 2008**

At a time of increased integration into the global economy and a celebration of the 'leap-frogging' of India into a global economy, such statistics about agriculturists are seen by many as a drag on the image of a nation that has ambitions of becoming a successful and powerful global player. Debates and discussions on the suicides and the limited media attention have often associated these suicides with increased indebtedness and the overall lack of development of agriculture in the nation. Neither purely economic analyses nor primarily psychological arguments are adequate to understanding the duration and spread of such a form of self-destruction, especially, among a people who have historically long suffered and weathered much privation and distress without resorting to such acts of desperation.

The suicides by agriculturists must not be seen only as markers of a 'crisis', a passing or temporary phenomenon in a nation undergoing rapid transition. Instead, what the suicides highlight are the production of desperate conditions in agrarian India which have resulted from the complexities of rural society in general, in agriculture as an economy in particular, and are abetted by a larger political economy of uncaring. The victims have been those who represent the majority of agriculturists: marginal and small cultivators whose average size of landholding is now (2011) only a mere 1.33 hectares. In the formation and manifestations of such distress, the suicides highlight the ways in which multiple features of the economy, society, and ecology have combined to make livelihoods untenable for a large proportion of people and for some, the most marginal and vulnerable cultivators, to consider such a life not worth living. Far from being only a crisis of transition from subsistence to commercial agriculture or signalling the pathetic psychological state of agriculturists, the suicides encapsulate the multiple tensions which mark the biography of the nation in its neo-liberal phase: in the privileging of the urban over the rural; the promotion of the market and the individual over the collective; in the erosion of long-evolved and locally embedded knowledge; and in the spread of multiple new risks that compound entrenched disadvantages.

Significant as the issue of suicide by agriculturists is in and of itself, it must be seen and understood in relation to the ongoing debates and trends in rural India, the agricultural economy, land, and agriculturists. Since the onset of full-fledged neo-liberal policies in 1991, rural and agricultural issues have been placed on the backburner of government policies and support. The rhetoric of agriculture being in a state of 'deceleration' since 1997, is often accompanied by a tone of resignation that sees the shift towards a non-agricultural economy and society as inevitable. Plans and policies which seek to induce or enforce industrialisation (as in the Singur and Nandigram cases which have become emblematic of government attempts to appropriate agricultural land) and the legitimisation of special economic zones (SEZs) draw on such rhetoric and ideas. This is compounded by market demand for land which has increasingly and very visibly rendered much of the land in the nation into a real estate grid, in which speculation and construction are key activities. While these have become policy-based trends, societal and political resistance against these have increased, taking the forms of violent encounters between residents, 'anti-state actors' and the armed wings of the State.

The persistence of the agrarian suicides over the years has enforced and has also become the reason for a range of new governmental initiatives that claim to ameliorate and alleviate rural distress but are in reality political strategies to appease an angry rural electorate. But despite the initiation of 'compensation' for families of the victims and the deployment of a range of 'relief schemes' – such as moratorium on institutional debts – the fact that suicides have continued indicates that the source of the problem and the deep structural roots of the distress – the overall neglect of agriculture and agriculturists – remain unaddressed. The oversight of the structural bases of agriculture and rural societies for much of the reform period (1991-2004) is now (since 2005) being sought to be readdressed by casting rural residents as voters who must be appeased with populist measures. What has followed such populist programmes is the constitution of the rural as a new, frontier market for consumer goods and for rural residents to be targeted as new consumers of a booming economy. Neglected in all these are the very structures of agriculture, the models and practices of agricultural production, and the capabilities of the majority of cultivators who are marginal to the dominant system. All of these point to the need to understand the predicament of rural India in the context of a dualistic economy; an accelerating global, urban, service economy and a decelerating, rural, agricultural economy. What needs to be discerned are how the specificities of varied regional, rural social structures and cultures are intertwined with the new economy and politics to render significant shifts in the life worlds of the people and in the very meaning of life in rural India.

The suicides represent not only the unresolved 'agrarian question' (how must land be used, what should be the model of agricultural development etc.) of a post-colonial India but also a plethora of associated questions that pertains to rural India itself. Attendant and pressing questions relate to the rights to land for the working poor (typically the share-croppers, tenants, landless, and low-ranked caste groups), the Adivasi or tribals, and women. A related and significant issue that remains is the problem of the type or model of agriculture that is relevant for India. Should the Green Revolution model of agriculture, which draws on a formula of enhanced capital, new technologies, alien knowledge, and is based on defying ecological specificities of agriculture be the foundation for all agricultural practices? What stands out explicitly in these cases of suicide, in the overall conditions of distress, and in the disenchantment with agriculture that large numbers of agriculturists are expressing, is the need to review and promote practices and patterns of agriculture that are suitable to the ecological, economic and social needs of the population. These suicides can also be seen as a form of structural violence in rural India, manifested in the continued poverty, erosion of livelihoods, and in the persistence and spread of continued degradation of the lives of the low-ranked, working caste groups and women.

Over the years, the nature of suicides itself has changed; from silent, individualised acts undertaken in the privacy of their homes or land, to recent ones in which whole families have committed suicide, to groups of agriculturists threatening or attempting to commit suicide in public, and to those in which agriculturists have addressed letters to the Prime Minister, Chief Minister and to their local political representatives, indicating the reasons for their dire action. In as much as suicides among agriculturists have gained a new-found cultural legitimacy, they have become significant political acts by which agriculturists signal not merely their own degraded condition but also the general deterioration in rural India, the very state of deceleration of agriculture and the agriculturists' eroded sense of agency and the loss of significance of life itself.

I first attempted to study suicides by undertaking field-work to understand the subjective and objective conditions which constituted and lcd to such deaths. In 1998, at the first spate of suicides in Bidar district in Karnataka, I met and interviewed some families and documented the 'agrarian distress' in a short study. But, the continued suicides and their intensity in 2004 compelled me to visit some other areas. As I undertook a household survey and visited families in the districts of Mandya and Hassan in Karnataka, I felt increasingly uncomfortable and awkward. If listening to the stories of hardships and struggles was harrowing, the inability to meet the expectations of those I talked with posed a bigger problem. Most members of the victims' families either requested that something be done to expedite their compensation or sought ways from me to alleviate their distress. Only some openly questioned what I or they would gain by this study. Convictions of the value of social research and the importance of the objectivity of the researcher failed to harden me to their desperate conditions. I thought I had no right to be there: asking questions for research purposes which, in all probability, will not resolve their plight. Following this, I abandoned plans to do extended case studies based on direct interactions with families of the victims, and over the years (2004-2009) collected all the studies, reports, discussions, and news pertaining to the suicides. A conversation with the anthropologist, Jean Comaroff, assured me that ethnography is not always the most appropriate method for socio-anthropological research for all contexts and issues and that one had to evolve and develop other methods to study such a situation.

Drawing on various studies and reports for the five states – Andhra Pradesh, Maharashtra, Karnataka, Punjab, and Kerala which account for the largest proportions of recorded suicides in the first phase (1997-2000) – I situate them in the larger socio-cultural and political-economic conditions and trends in the nation and then read these for their sociological significance. Although suicides by agriculturists have been reported, since 2008, from Madhya Pradesh, Chhattisgarh, and Gujarat, there are no formal reports and studies from these regions and the state governments continue to deny these trends. Hence, details from these three states have not been integrated into the study but the conditions and trends can be generalised to these regions as well.

This book draws on ideas from earlier essays (Vasavi 1999, 2009) but I have re-worked the approach to the issue and have qualified some interlinkages between the macro economic and political factors and the sociological understanding of the suicides as social acts. While I draw on primary and secondary data about the families, I present the suicides as acts that result from the coalescence of a combination of structural factors, trends, events, and ideas and from the people's subjective experience of their conditions. Hence, this study is not focused primarily on the suicides but is an attempt to see the suicides as windows to understand conditions and trends in rural India. In doing so, I interlink the external vectors of the macro national, political economy with the new burdens and risks of Green Revolution agriculture. I then draw on details of the conditions of marginalised agricultural households (representing most of the victims), and the new social and cultural registers of rural society to locate the contexts and conditions (and not necessarily the personal reasons) for agriculturists to resort to suicide.

Typically, literature on agrarian issues refers to 'peasants' as those who cultivate primarily for subsistence, and to 'farmers' as those who engage with the market and who undertake commercial cultivation.

In preferring to use the term 'agriculturist', I seek to encapsulate and represent all cultivators who either engage in production for subsistence (or only for their own and family's needs) and/or for the market and who occupy a range of positions from that of cultivators-cum-labourers to those who are landlords. This term also enables me to avoid the pejorative resonance that the term 'peasant' has and the association with commercial or market production that the term 'farmer' has. In many ways the term agriculturist is also closer to the varied regional words, *kisan*, *ryot*, *raitha*, *ryatlu*, *shetkari*, etc., which are used by agriculturists themselves.

I frame the varied details about rural India by seeking to answer key questions related to the suicides: How were these suicides viewed against the larger narrative of the nation's fast growing, new economy? (Chapter I); why have these deaths occurred in rural India, therefore what are the emerging structures of India's ruralities? (Chapter II); what are the key features of agriculture that have enhanced the risk load of agriculturists? (Chapter III); what are the household/family and social conditions of marginal agriculturists which dispose them to high levels of vulnerability? (Chapter IV); why have these conditions of distress not been adequately addressed by the State and why have agriculturists, despite the onset of intense forms of distress and the suicides, not resorted to political and other forms of mobilisation? (Chapter V); and finally, what are the implications of all these trends and conditions for the predicament of rural India in the twenty-first century? (Chapter VI). In attempting to answer these questions, I draw on six inter-related concepts or ideas/arguments. The first chapter provides a summary snapshot of the reports of suicides by agriculturists from various states and indicates the key historical and sociological questions that need to be posed in order to understand their significance. I consider the reporting of the suicides, the responses from the State, civil society organisations, and by agriculturists also as indicating the extent to which the suicides occupy a 'shadow space' in the narratives of the nation. Denied any structural significance, the suicides are seen as aberrations that mar the making of a globalising India. The second chapter provides a broad overview of the state of contemporary rurality. Focusing on rurality as a broad geo-physical and socio-economic and political space, rather than only on villages and/or on agriculture, I seek to highlight the emergent structures of India's rurality. In demarcating this space as such, the study tries to locate the broader political-economic and cultural processes through which rurality in general and agriculturists in particular have been impacted. In focusing on the retention of caste as a key structuring force, I elaborate on ways in which caste-based rights to resources and power are largely reproduced despite the introduction of 'modern' forms of economy and polity. In Chapter III I elaborate on the economic, ecological and social implications of multiple and interlinked risks that most agriculturists face under the regime of the Green Revolution and especially now, during neo-liberal times. In Chapter IV, I highlight the specific economic and social conditions of small and marginal agriculturists and I indicate how individualisation of agriculture and the social entrapment of marginal agriculturists compound their vulnerability and subsequently lead to the loss of their sense of agency, thereby making suicide an alternative exit to their hard-pressed lives.

In delineating the reasons for the political and economic neglect of the rural and hence of the issues of suicides itself, in Chapter V, I highlight the multiple ways in which rural India has been subject to processes of marginalisation and thereby to a general retrogression of the rural in the political-economic agendas and the social imaginaries of those who govern India. The combined impact of all processes and trends is considered, in Chapter VI, to lead to forms of 'involution' where the retention of established structures has combined with new forces and forms to produce multiple forms of violence. Such an involution accounts for the range of violence against the working poor, and for the emergence of trends and conditions that render democracy, modernity, and development complex and problematic. The study concludes with a commentary on the significance of the suicides not only for agriculturists and for rural India but also for the nation as a whole. Given the gravity of the issue and with the intention of broad-basing discussions related to the state of rural India, I have chosen to write this for a wide and interested audience rather than for a primarily academic one. Interested readers may peruse the details and qualifying arguments that are provided in the end notes to each chapter.

Finally, it behoves all of us to recognise that the trajectory of rural India is more closely aligned with the life and career of the nation as a whole than is made out to be. The rural and the agricultural, despite forecasts of imminent disappearance and death, remain the bedrock of life in India and therefore of the life of the nation.

Does the *Sarkar* not know that our household head has been swallowed by burdens of agriculture? How must we show our loss.... of our elder, of the crops, the growing loans?

Rangappa, brother of a suicide victim, Hassan district, Karnataka

How many deaths does it take to be known that too many people have died?

Bob Dylan

Chapter One

Suicides as Shadow Space

Only foolish farmers commit suicide.
Agricultural Officer, Chhattisgarh, 2008

It starts with a trickle of news from various parts of the country. In 1997, a farmer, Ramdas Ambavar, in the dry belt of the Vidarbha region in Maharashtra, commits suicide unable to pay his loans. In Andhra Pradesh's Warangal district, agriculturists begin to pay the price for switching to cotton cultivation. Prolonged rains, spurious seeds and pesticides see an outbreak of pests in the plants and agriculturists watch their crops wilt and much of the standing crops destroyed. Reports of suicides trickle through the media and by the end of the winter season of 1997 it is a harvest of deaths and not of the expected bounty of 'white gold'. In the neighbouring state of Karnataka, agriculturists in the district of Bidar agonise as their crops of red gram are eaten by an outbreak of the *heliotheses* pest and in the villages of Bilgi taluk twenty-two agriculturists, including a woman, commit suicide. From the heart of India's 'grain bowl', Punjab, unbelievable reports come of the once sturdy agriculturists committing suicide in the districts of Sangrur and Mansa.[1] In the mountainous belts of Idukki and Wayanad in Kerala, news spreads of the crash in prices of coffee, tea, cardamom, pepper, and vanilla. At first, the distress sales of land by marginal cultivators increase and then between the years of 2000-2007, there are 371 suicides by agriculturists in the plantation belts of Kerala.[2] Between 1997 and March 2008, Maharashtra alone records a total of forty-one thousand, four hundred and four suicides by agriculturists.

As prices for the crops of gram and soya collapse, marginal agriculturists in Hoshangabad, Vidisha, and Sihor districts in Madhya Pradesh who had taken to cultivating soya and rapeseeds start to commit suicide either by hanging or poisoning themselves.[3] From Chhattisgarh's Durg district come reports of suicides by hanging and poisoning. But the officials of the state governments, in both Chhattisgarh and Madhya Pradesh, go into denial. "Only idiot farmers commit suicide" asserts one agricultural officer for Chhattisgarh, when confronted with details about suicides.[4] Even as the report by the National Crime Records Bureau (2008) points out that the total number of suicides in Madhya Pradesh and Chhattisgarh has increased alarmingly, there are no official reports, assessments or discussions about the situation. News circulate about agriculturists committing suicides in Gujarat, but the Chief Minister, Narendra Modi, riding a wave of mass popularity and promoting the state as 'vibrant Gujarat', an investor friendly state, says that "Gujarat's farmers are not like those in other states. Our farmers drive Maruti cars".[5]

The suicides take on additional dimensions. From reports of single members, typically family heads, committing suicide there are now reports of whole families committing suicide. Family homicide and suicide combine in some villages. In Punjab's Sakraudi village, a "heavily indebted Kuljit Singh killed his wife and teenage son with a machete and then committed suicide by consuming a poisonous fumigant" (Newman 2007: 5). The report by the 'Commission on Farmers' Welfare' points out that "agriculture in Andhra Pradesh is in an advanced state of crisis" (2005:12). Over the years, the suicides gain intensity and spread. Bothbodan village, inhabited only by members of the Banjara community, of Yavatmal district in Maharashtra, is subject to multiple suicides. In a village of a hundred odd households, eighteen families report suicides of family members, all of which are related to agricultural indebtedness. Members of the new National Commission for Farmers,[6] set up by the government of India, and led by the renowned agricultural scientist, Dr. M.S. Swaminathan, visit villages in the Vidarbha belt, now declared as the 'suicide belt' of the country and decry the lack of infrastructure and investment in agriculture. And in Sangrur district in the Punjab, some families face multiple suicides – of father, brothers, cousins, and uncles – all earning members who sought to escape the load of indebtedness and their inability to sustain their families.

On September 6, 2007, the journalist, P. Sainath, who has been reporting consistently and with great depth on the distress in various parts of the country, delivers a lecture to members of the Parliament. He speaks of the emergency in the rural areas and asks the members to recognise that, "We, as a nation, are in the worst agrarian crisis in four decades. … the crisis is so deep, so advanced …the suicides are merely, however tragic, just a symptom and not the disease. They are a consequence, not the process"(2007b: 2). As desperation and despondency spread, twelve families from Punjab, which have suffered from debt-related suicides in the family, gather together in New Delhi in February 2008, to petition the government and seek compensation and support for their dependent children

A decade since the start of the suicides, comes news that there are now agrarian suicides from many more Indian states.[7] In village Kaimi Bhood of Lakhipur district in Uttar Pradesh, two brothers who were forced to auction their lands to repay old debts, commit suicide in December 2007. Deaths resulting from excessive agriculture-related debts are reported from Rajasthan in December 2009.[8] Between the months of September and December 2009, forty families in Sambalpur district in Orissa resort to suicide. In West Bengal's Burdwan district, there are reports of suicides by two agriculturists, who have incurred heavy losses after the crash in potato prices. The state government faces threats by more agriculturists to commit suicide and with demands for higher support prices.[9]

Demands in the legislative assemblies in the states, expressions of concern by imminent citizens, the establishment of people's enquiry commissions, and reports by a range of civil society organisations and non-government organisations seek to bring more attention and relief to the distressed agricultural sector. The Forum on Social and Human Rights, in Andhra Pradesh, seeks the immediate intervention of the Prime Minister, Manmohan Singh, to prevent the suicide of farmers in Andhra Pradesh. During public hearings on the suicides, conducted by the Concerned Citizens' Forum, debt worn agriculturists depose before the audience of eminent persons, highlighting their growing indebtedness and the unviability of the new agricultural policies. On news of the suicides in the Wayanad belt, the National Human Rights Commission issues a notice to the Kerala Government seeking a report on the increasing number of suicides by farmers. The Vidarbha Jan Andolan Samiti (Vidarbha People's Movement Committee), led by Kishor Tiwari, provides daily counts of the suicides in the hinterland of the Vidarbha belts. Taking to writing a blog, Tiwari chastises the government, the politicians and the media for not recognizing the crisis and demands the provisioning of food security to small cultivators and landless labourers. The Karnataka Rajya Raitha Sangha suddenly springs into action and seeks to reactivate itself and its presence in Karnataka through is own fact-finding committees and the publication of reports.[10] A new outfit, the Karnataka Raitara Atmahatya Nigrah Dal (Karnataka Farmers' Suicide Prevention Squad) comes into being, demanding that the government provide compensation to the families of those who have committed suicide in the agricultural belt. Mata Amritanandamayi, known as the 'hugging mother', a spiritual leader and icon, travels to Ahmednagar in the Vidarbha belt and speaks about the distress. "In truth", she asserts, "the situation is worse than a Third World War. If it were war, there would be instant death – not this long drawn out suffering". She calls for the 'spiritual strengthening' of people and announces scholarships for children orphaned by parental suicides.[11]

The families of farmers, who committed suicide in the drought-prone Rayalseema region of Andhra Pradesh, meet members of the Planning Commission on December 29, 2004, and narrate conditions in their drought-hit villages. They note how farmers' suicides due to falling water levels, failing crops and high indebtedness are taking its toll on village women who are now recruited to brothels in Pune and Mumbai.[12] By 2005, growing mobilisation by civil society groups and the persistence of suicides in the Vidarbha belt become a glaring national issue, forcing the Prime Minister to declare a "package to rehabilitate the farmers of the Vidarbha". The parliamentary elections of 2004, read as a vote against the marginalisation of rural and agricultural issues, forces the dominant political party to promulgate and deploy a range of programmes from 2005 onwards to alleviate agricultural distress. Economic packages to supposedly alleviate indebtedness and distress are announced first for select regions and then a national level agricultural debt moratorium plan is deployed. A major employment guarantee programme, under the National Rural Employment Guarantee Act, is promulgated and passed in the parliament. Yet, the suicides continue in the belts.

A delegation of 'Family Members of Farmers who have Committed Suicide in Gujarat' makes a round of meetings, first with the leader of the Congress Party, Mrs. Sonia Gandhi, then with members of the Planning Commission and then with the press, in New Delhi on October 11, 2007. The main speaker, Bharat Jhala, highlights for his audience the numbers and conditions of suicides in Gujarat. Based on information, that was reluctantly and after much persistence delivered to him under his RTI (Right to Information) application, he finds that a total of 403 farmers in Gujarat have committed suicide between the periods of 2003-2007. The suicide toll is first from Junagadh followed by those in Rajkot, Jamnagar and Mehsana. More drastic is the fact that the state government, celebrating its growing clout as a developed and pro-industry state, denies the suicides and refuses to disburse any compensation.[13] On December 18, 2009, members of the Nagarika Samaj take out a procession in Bhubaneshwar, Orissa, calling attention to the deaths of agriculturists in the state. The Krishak Mahasangh then files a Public Interest Litigation (PIL) case in the high court, seeking a report on the causes of suicides by agriculturists and demanding that the state provide some compensation to the victims' families.

Meanwhile, Sharad Pawar, an agriculturist turned politician, and the nation's Agriculture Minister for a second round,[14] spends more time discussing and organizing the Indian cricket board. Challenged by journalists and at public meetings, he seeks to deny and thereby overlook the intensity of the crisis in the rural areas. "Suicides are not restricted to one sector of the society", he asserts and, dismissing the deaths, calls for reducing the dependency on agriculture and initiating new alternatives for livelihoods. Although there are hopes of starting a new year without suicides in the agrarian belts, Madhya Pradesh witnesses the death of several agriculturists in the month of January 2011. And, far from commiserating with the deaths, the Minister for Agriculture issues a statement noting,[15] "The farmers are paying for their past sins of making fertile land barren by excessive use of fertilisers and pesticides".

Even as small newspapers and local media report these suicides, they are unacknowledged by the larger national press. Suicides continue over the years of 2010 and 2011 in Karnataka, in Maharashtra, in Madhya Pradesh, Andhra Pradesh, and Chhattisgarh. Even as unrelenting news and disclosures of rampant and high levels of corruption – in the distortion of bids for communication networks, in the construction of megacomplexes for the commonwealth games, in the role of the lobbies and elite journalists in politics – become matrix events in the public life of the nation, individual suicides by agriculturists are no longer considered newsworthy. And, bursting on the scene, on February 5, 2011, comes news of twelve agriculturists from Gulbarga district, Karnataka, attempting to commit mass suicide in the premises of the tehsildar as their demand for remunerative prices for red gram went unattended.

Agrarian Suicides as Shadow Space

In the making of this theatre of distress, the news about the suicides, significant when read by themselves, are not sustained issues of interest in the mainstream media, the political processes, and the articulations of public policy for the nation. The gravity of the situation, the intensifying distress, the spread, and the pleas to address the situation are largely dismissed by the dominant political, economic, and media players. The trickle of news, rarely mentioned or discussed on most of the newly proliferating satellite-based television channels, is increasingly consigned to a shadow space.[16] When the suicides do become newsworthy they are spread in various forms: sometimes as sensational news; sometimes as spectacles from moribund rural areas; most often as small print items that receive space grudgingly in some daily newspapers; and rarely as events that reveal the desperate lives of the majority agrarian community. In many narratives and reports of the suicides, agriculturists and the conditions of the agrarian belts are represented in tones of pathos, as attributes of a helpless and inert population of agriculturists,[17] and of the inevitable redundancy of the large rural population. More pointedly, the suicides do not become the bases for questioning economic policies, the programmes of development, and the practices of administration. Official reports seek reasons and causes and many identify the problems with the agriculturists themselves. The causes or factors become dis-aggregated and placed under piecemeal analyses in official reports that mark the suicide in terms of 'real distress' or 'linked to family conditions', 'poor mental health', and/or to personal 'inadequacies' and 'problems' such as 'alcoholism', and 'indebtedness for drugs and consumerism'. The staple response of the government ranges from complete disregard to partially ameliorative and populist programmes, and not comprehensive policies to address the structural bases of the deficits of the agrarian structure. The root causes remain unaddressed, the victims and the vulnerable continue to remain in conditions of distress, and the suicides continue apace.

Unfolding in a shadow space, the suicides, representing the economic 'deceleration of agriculture' and the degraded conditions of agriculturists, have become a counter narrative to the dominant narrative of a booming, urban and globalising economy. Between the years of 1997-2000, the news and details of the suicides were represented as a noise amidst the heralding of a 'new India', in which the emerging Information Technology (IT) economy was to catalyse the rest of the nation towards high economic growth. Government engagement with the news was to either deny the problems in the agrarian sector or to defer any policy review that warranted a critical look at the rural and the agricultural sectors. In 2004, even when the numbers of suicides by agriculturists reached a peak of a total of 18,241 at the all-India level, the information remained a footnote, a black mark that spoilt the new track record of the nation. Even as the spectres of crop loss, indebtedness, and continuing suicides spread across states and regions, corporate leaders and international financial powers welcomed India to the high table of economic power. India was widely recognised as another rising power and was associated with Brazil, Russia and China as one of the new economic giants. Key players of the global market, PriceWaterHouseCoopers (PwC), the Confederation of Indian Industries (CII), and the National Association for Software and Services Companies (NASSCOM) celebrated the high economic growth rates that have the potential to overcome the doomed 'Hindu Rate of Growth' and which were speeding India on to the road to superpowerdom. New industrial and corporate icons joined the pantheon of film and cricket celebrities and much of the print and burgeoning television media paid no heed to the deaths in the rural belts. If the globalizing economy of new service industries and booming manufacturing were about to change the long history of deprivation in the nation, then the suicides were the new blight that threatened an emergent, 'shining India'.

Consigning the suicides and all details associated with them to a shadow space mean that the conditions, trends and life-worlds of rural India are all placed under a framework of aberration – where the conditions and structures of agriculture and the agency of agriculturists become the problem itself. More troubling, in consigning the suicides to a shadow space, the State and its machinery seek to render and treat not only the victims but all rural residents, especially agriculturists as 'distant strangers' (Bauman: 2001:25) – not merely as those about whom little was known but as those whose details are no longer of interest to the nation. The reaction to the suicides, the lack of genuine public and governmental engagement with the issues, and the persistent failure to address the problems are similar to the ways in which the wars in Afghanistan and Iraq have been normalised and made acceptable to the larger world community. "The de-realisation of loss – the insensitivity to human suffering and death – becomes the mechanism through which dehumanisation is accomplished. This de-realisation takes place neither inside nor outside the image, but through the very framing in which the image is contained" (Butler 2004: 148).

Dominant Explanations for the Phenomenon of Suicides in the Agrarian Belts

Several government reports, studies and documentation by non-government organisations and activists on the suicides have identified the larger factors that account for the onset of such distress. Some of the key structural issues that have been identified are: the impact of neo-liberal economic policies, including the integration of Indian agriculture into the world market (Shiva and Jafri 1998; Patnaik 2004, 2006; Walker 2008); increasing costs of agricultural production (Mohanty and Shroff 2004; Vyas 2004); inadequate institutional support including lack of availability of credit and deceleration in agricultural growth (Dev 2004, Ghosh 2004; Rao and Gopalappa 2004; Vaidyanathan 2006; RBI 2006; Reddy and Mishra 2009); as well as decline in wages, growing indebtedness and unemployment, and frequent loss of agricultural crops (Dev 2004; Patnaik 2004; Sarma 2004). Studies that have explicated primarily macro and micro economic factors overlook the fact that local, non-economic factors have also played a significant role in abetting suicide. While the decline in prices of commodities such as cotton and spices have been linked to globalisation and the opening up of the market, several cases of suicides are related to the production of commercial crops (primarily that of pulses, wheat, rice) that have not been affected by international prices (see GoI report 2007). Similarly, although the introduction of Bt cotton has and continues to play a largely negative role in some pockets such as that of the Vidarbha region in parts of Maharashtra, the report by the International Food Policy Research Institute (Guere et al. 2008) is correct to indicate that introduction of Bt cotton is not the key or singular factor responsible for suicides by agriculturists. Neither has drought been the sole reason, over the past thirteen years (1997-2010), for the distress and loss experienced by agriculturists in the five different regions and states. While indebtedness, related to crop production and to investments in land, is one of the important factors, it is not an unusual condition as Indian agriculture and agriculturists have a long record of usury and indebtedness being a key and negative force in their lives.

Over the years, the narratives that have sought to highlight the persistence and spread of the agrarian suicides have also suggested that such suicides have become an 'epidemic'. Yet identifying these suicides as an epidemic would be to naturalise the incidents and to be as dismissive of the suicides as have been the many governments, most policy makers, and the media. To go beyond the simplistic and dismissive diagnoses that most government-nominated committees have made, it is imperative that we see these suicides by agriculturists as social acts signalling their position/condition in the context of significant re-structuring and re-orientation of the economic, political, ecological, and socio-cultural domains in agricultural societies and in the rural areas. Contextualising these suicides on a larger canvas calls for a critical review of this spate of suicides which can provide "a politicised orientation to our respective dead" (Hudson 2002: 26). These deaths must be understood in their historical and contemporaneous perspectives. If the famine deaths of the late nineteenth century, including those in colonial India, are the 'late Victorian Holocausts' (Davis 2001), then how must these deaths, triggered at the end of the twentieth century, gaining spread and volume in the first decade of the twenty-first century, be seen, represented and remembered?

In many ways, the sheer numbers, the spread, and the overall distress linked to the model of agriculture and the agrarian social structure make these suicides akin to the famines of the British colonial period. If the recurring famines during the British colonial rule highlighted, as nationalists repeatedly pointed out, the complete depredation of the rural economy (Stokes 1978), then these contemporary suicides in the rural hinterland stand as testimonials to the further degradation of rural India and its marginal cultivators.

More specifically, these deaths by suicide were and are preventable as were the mass deaths by starvation in the colonial period. Yet, a key question that these suicides pose pertains to the inability or the failure of agriculturists to rise up against the onset and impact of such severe forms of distress. If historically periods of agrarian transition have led to riots[18] (Swing riots of 1830s in England, Deccan riots of 1870s in Western India), rebellion (as in Russia in the 1860s), and to revolution (as in China in 1940s) and to forms of resistance (as in various parts of Latin America), then what accounts for this nearly silent form of self-destruction? To understand the reasons for this key contradiction, it is important to view the suicides as social acts which derive their logic and reason from the very fabric of rural Indian society and to assess the impact of the forms of continuity and change that constitute it.

Cultural Bases of Suicides?

Since the overwhelming number of victims were Hindus it is important to contextualise the cultural bases of these suicides and their significance. Suicide in Hindu society and culture occupies an ambivalent position. On the one hand, classic texts proscribe suicide and the very etymology of suicide as *atmahatya* (killing of soul) or *atmaghataka* (destruction of soul) highlights this; but the emphasis on a cycle of births and deaths makes taking one's life an ambiguous act (Ruzika 1998). Bodies of suicide victims are not entitled to receive the standard rituals of cremation. On the other hand, texts such as the *Ramayana* and *Mahabharata* are also replete with instances of suicide that are represented as heroic acts (Thakur 1963). Rama, the revered hero of the *Ramayana*, himself commits suicide by walking into the Sarayu river as do several others in the numerous stories and sub-stories of the two epics. Forms of suicide such as *sati*[19] (immolation by widows), *jauhar* (group suicide by women in the face of abduction or loss of honour), and the Jaina form of *samlekhana* (death by withholding food and water) are well-known forms of self death (Mody 2007) that are culturally recognised and accepted.[20] Historical records are replete with instances of kings and queens of the medieval period resorting to suicide as a way to save their honour and prestige.

Suicide is prohibited and deprecated among most of the tribal societies in India[21] and as with classic Hindu texts, the bodies of those who have committed suicide are not honoured with regular burial ceremonies (Elwin 1943). But the prevalence of suicide itself has been noted and is associated as a way out of leprosy, illness, widowhood, jealousy, and insult. The ambivalence towards suicide is elaborated by Verrier Elwin for the Maria of Bastar, among whom he notes, "…suicide is a wretched deed; it certainly has no higher, hallowing significance: but it is no light or trivial matter due to lack of foresight" (1943: 57). But Elwin also indicates that suicide is accepted as a "way to restore honour" and as a form of "preserving dignity and prestige" (1943: 58).

Legally, suicide is considered a criminal offence and is based on the British colonial construction of suicide as signs of disaffection against the government and of its inability to provide order (Thakur 1963). Persons attempting suicide or those abetting others to suicide can be booked under the Indian Penal Code[22] (Section 305). Recording suicides as an offence accounts for the reason that data and statistics related to suicide are maintained in police records.[23] In fact, *satyagraha,* the form of political defiance that Gandhi developed and deployed as a form of moral and political protest draws on the idea of potential self-death acting as a moral load on violators (Thakur 1963).

The possibility of self death as a way to restore one's honour and/or to question larger distortions and deviations from order and morality form the bases of the cultural and religious roots of suicide as a political act. Suicide as a public phenomenon has had a presence in post-colonial India and has marked the varied lives and circumstances of different people. Potti Sriramulu's death in 1952 in Hyderabad by fasting for fifty one days was a political act to draw attention to the demand for a new state for Telugu-speaking people. Since then, over the years, public immolation of self as acts of protest against government policies and as forms of devotion to public icons has gained some currency. Various agitations, from that against the construction of the Narmada dam to those against caste-based reservation policies in education have invoked the possibility of public suicide as ritualised political acts.

Suicides have also been registered as periodically occurring 'epidemics'. One of the earliest and large-scale phenomenon of suicide was reported from the then Saurashtra area of Rajkot (now in Gujarat) where about 167 women committed suicide between the period of 1954-55 (Thakur 1963) and these were linked to marital problems. Since the 1960s, Kerala has recorded higher than national average levels of suicide and many of these, including the rash of family suicides, have been linked to higher aspiration levels with access to higher education but lack of commensurate employment opportunities and more recently to increasing indebtedness. Over the past two decades, 'epidemics of suicide' have gained momentum and are reported from the main metropolitan areas and are largely about adolescents and teenagers who face problems in examinations and are education-related issues. In some rural areas, such as in Tamil Nadu, suicides by youth who consume pesticides has also reached alarming levels (Zachariah 2010) and are largely linked to personal problems. Suicides also account for a large proportion of deaths of women, especially of those in the reproductive ages of 15 to 44 years (Mayer 2011). In terms of regions, Sikkim has registered high levels of suicide and Bangalore, among the metropolises, has recorded high levels of suicide, especially among youth. And recently since 2009, the agitation for a separate state, Telangana, has presented to us spectacles in which the key leader and several students have sought to commit suicide.

Yet, the suicides by agriculturists stand as a historical aberration. Despite a history associated with frequent agriculture related distress in pre-colonial and colonial India, there are no records of widespread suicides by agriculturists that in any way can be compared to those that have occurred since 1997. Reviews of historical responses to agrarian distress (Rana 2006) indicate that the agrarian crises of the seventeenth and eighteenth centuries in North India led to the abandonment of agriculture, widespread migration and even desertion of whole villages. But there is no mention of agriculturists resorting to suicide. The only record of a history of suicides related to agricultural distress is from the Bundelkhand region of Uttar Pradesh and was linked to the problems of indebtedness and loss of crops, in the late nineteenth century, when a group of agriculturists committed suicide (Siddiqi 1973). In contrast, these suicides in contemporary times have occurred when there are no conditions that are akin to that of famines in the late eighteenth and early nineteenth centuries. In fact, it is important to note that these suicides have occurred during a period of unprecedented economic boom in the nation and have been seen as anomalous to expectations that the urban boom would spread to the village and to the agricultural sector. That this trickle down and multiplier effect of the liberalised economic growth has not happened and suicides by agriculturists stand as a sign of the 'ill-fare' (Harriss-White 1999) of agriculturists requires us to understand the state and predicament of rural India.

Out of the Shadow Space to Sociological Scrutiny

If suicide as a way out of agricultural distress and of heavy indebtedness has no established historical and social record then the question is why agriculture-related indebtedness itself has suddenly become so overbearing a burden. To remove the suicides from the shadow space that they have been consigned to is to engage with several inter-related questions. Instead of seeking to identify either a causal chain or a linear causality between 'proximate and root causes' (ideas that have gained common parlance in many of the official fact-finding reports) of suicide, I focus on understanding the constellation of multiple factors and the links between the macro political and economic conditions and the local contexts in which such distress has been produced. I anchor this constellation of factors and forces to certain conjunctural situations in the social life of the agriculturists, which at the level of each individual produces intense distress and the desire to die.

In proposing an integrated socio-cultural approach[24] to understanding these suicides, I also seek to go beyond the standard, and now even commonsensical, understanding of the Durkheimian approach to suicide as resulting from either anomic, egoistic, or altruistic links to society[25] as the social, historical and cultural constitution of these suicides is vastly different from the suicides of nineteenth century Europe.[26] Emphasising the relational dimensions of the reasons for suicides is to recognise that "suicidal actions almost always mean something fundamental both about the person and about the situation of the person: each is seen…as a 'cause' of the suicidal action" (Douglas 1967: 251). Jaworski's recent work on suicide also endorses such a perspective and argues for recognizing suicide as a 'performative act' to be read as "a reiterative and citational practice, made possible through norms, meanings, assumptions, and knowledges identified within existing historical conditions and patterns, through which something about the act can be hailed and understood as a deliberate taking of one's life" (Jaworksi 2010: 680).

The situational meanings and relational approaches to understanding suicides do not completely override Durkheim's contribution in asserting linkages between the individual and the social structure and in moving understandings of suicide away from the then prevailing moral, psychological, and physiological arguments. Indeed, Durkheim's insights and arguments compel us to acknowledge the relationship of social actions to the social structure (Giddens 1968). These broad sociological interlinkages need to be contextualised with the cultural scripts by which the victims had related to their circumstances and the discourse by which members of the victims' families and communities/villages understand and relate to these events. Doing so is to highlight the affective dimensions that constitute the subjectivities by which the victims lived their lives (Fullagar 2003).

Contemporary trends indicate that a range of new types of suicides have gained mainstay all over the world. These include forms such as familicide-cum suicide, honour suicides, copycat suicides, cult suicides, forced suicides, internet suicides, mass murder-suicide, etc.[27] Increasing suicides all over the world have become a matter of concern and according to the World Health Organisation (2000), suicides account for one of the single biggest non-natural causes of death. Sharp shifts in economic conditions in the South-East and Asian Pacific region (Ruzika, 1998; WHO 2000; Denton 2000; Macdonald 2003), as also in Africa (Livingston 2009) have made several groups and classes of people vulnerable to suicide and to unusual forms of violence. Going beyond the predominantly economic causes that are associated with suicides (that is as related to increased indebtedness or heavy losses in production), a sociological commentary requires us to locate the suicides on multiple levels and subject both primary and secondary data to scrutiny.

In international assessments and comparisons, India occupies a middle rank in suicide mortality rates (SMR) [1999 data: 11.2 for India; highest SMR: Lithuania at 38.4; and lowest: Syrian Arab Republic 0.1] but given the size of the population, it accounts for the second highest, after China, for the total numbers of suicides (Mayer 2011). That the suicides by agriculturists since 1997 are significant and are not normal or average data for the population as a whole or for the agricultural population is evident from the trends. Data for the decade 1997-2006 indicates that the year 1998 itself recorded an eighteen per cent increase in the total number of suicides. In 1997, a total of 13,622 agriculturists were reported as having committed suicide at the all-India level and the number had increased to 17,060 at the end of 2006. Of these the numbers committing suicide in the five key states indicated an increase of sixty per cent (1997 recorded 7,236 suicides by agriculturists and the figures rose to 11,638 in 2006). By 2001, nearly 13 per cent of all suicides were by agriculturists and was higher than the national suicide mortality rate (SMR) of 10.6 for a population of one hundred thousand. By 2002, the suicide mortality rate had increased to that of 16.3 among agriculturists while it was 10.5 persons among non-agriculturists. Suicides by male agriculturists were 30 per cent higher than the general male population.[28] In addition, local records and reports from specific areas where the suicides were reported indicate dramatic increases in the deaths by suicide in these areas (Vasavi 1999; Citizens' Report 1998; Karulkar 2006). Adjusted for population size, Meeta and Rajivlochan (2006) assess that the suicide rates in Yavatmal district of Maharashtra for the period of 2004 was 300 per cent more than that for Mumbai in the same period.

In gaining epidemic levels in specific areas and zones and in their volume, intensity, spread, and significance the suicides are social facts. As social facts the suicides encapsulate and represent key structures, ideas, norms, and trends about the society in which they are occurring. The contexts in which suicides are committed, the range of meanings associated with them by the families and those in the immediate society of the suicide victims have gained new meaning and call attention to the socio-cultural and political significance that the suicides have gained. Local discussions about the incidence of suicides in the villages have become discursive narratives in which people review the life of the person who committed suicide, the situation in the village and the burdens of being in agriculture.

A comparative perspective, linking these suicides to trends at international levels, indicates that suicide rates for agriculturists have over the years, especially since 1980s, become higher than for non-rural and non-agricultural groups. Since the 1990s suicides by agriculturists have been reported from countries including the United States, United Kingdom and in several countries of Europe and the South-East Asia.[29] In the U.S., a predominantly agricultural state such as Oklahoma recorded high levels of suicide among farmers (Ramirez-Ferrero 2005) between 2000-2003. What such trends, including those in India, require us to engage with are the linkages between conditions of households, communities, capital, knowledge, labour, social aspirations, and market. In the making of suicides as 'epidemics' in certain regions and the intensity and spread in specific times, what we are witness to are the ways in which even distant policies have both secondary and immediate effects on widely varied populations and on the life conditions and subjectivity of people.

Given such broad and comparative trends in the making of suicides, what needs to be emphasised is not the cultural tendency or specificity of resorting to suicides as much as the situational conditions that make suicide a culturally acceptable social act which then spreads among people. Focusing on the configurations which constitute the situation and in reading the meanings of these situations and the cultural scripts by which people understand and come to terms with the suicides require us to pose the following questions: Why did the suicides take place in the rural areas and why was it primarily among marginalised agriculturists who had taken to commercial cultivation of crops? Responding to these questions raises further questions: what are the conditions or characteristics of contemporary rural India and its economic and political contexts and situations? Linked to this, what are the processes of agricultural production in the key areas from which suicides have been reported? What are the conditions of the marginal cultivators who were the predominant victims? What were the cultural scripts surrounding the act of suicide? And finally, what is the larger economic, political and social significance of the suicides for agriculture as a domain and for agriculturalists as key national actors? Attempting to provide such a perspective requires one to move away from the shadow space to which the suicides have been consigned and to review the deaths and the reasons behind them which are in reality the entrenched structural problems of rural and agrarian India.

Triggered exactly after fifty years of Independence (1947-1997), and at the close of the twentieth century, the suicides can be yardsticks by which to assess and review conditions in rural India and the lives of the people who live there. The suicides compel us to question not only the trajectory of 'development' that has been deployed in rural India but to also highlight the multiple ways in which the lives of the marginalised and the disadvantaged have become fragile and untenable. In sum, these suicides urge us to review the persistence of entrenched structures and processes of disadvantage in rural economic production and socio-cultural and political reproduction, and to review the contradictions posed by issues such as the linkages and tensions between agriculture and industrialisation, between environmental conservation and economic growth, between local/indigenous knowledge and modern, dominant science and technology.

Key questions that arise relate to the very characteristics of rural India, to the dominant model and practice of agriculture, and to the lives of those who are marginal in the whole configuration. In providing a window through which to understand the contemporary trends and predicament of rural India, the suicides call for a critical appraisal of India's rural and agrarian societies and the patterns and forms of changes that have taken place there. In this re-look and review we will see that the rural and the village bear only some resemblance to the established images of the 'village India' of old, and the key actors are no longer just subsistence 'peasants' but are citizens with higher levels of aspirations who are seeking an entry into the market and to the promises and potential that it holds.

Notes

1 Gill and Singh (2006) indicate that the suicides in the agricultural belts of Punjab had started in the 1980s and that they gained momentum in the late 1990s.

2 All data and details related to the incidence of suicide across the eight states are drawn from official reports, newspaper reports, and studies. The following have been the key official reports for the various states: for Punjab IDC (1998), and Iyer and Manick (2000); Karnataka (Government of Karnataka 2002), Andhra Pradesh (Commission on Farmers' Welfare 2005), and for Maharashtra (Dandekar et al. 2005); Mishra (2006). Some of the reports by various commissions set up by independent agriculturists groups (e.g. for Andhra Pradesh the ones by the Citizens' Committee (1998) and the Farmers Commission of Experts (2002),Christian Aid (Christian Aid 2005). Data for Madhya Pradesh, Chhattisgarh, and Gujarat have been scanty and were sourced from reports, notes and additional materials sent in by persons such as Sudhanshu Choudhury of Chhattisgarh, Sachin Jain of Vikas Samvaad of Madhya Pradesh, Bharat Jhala of Gujarat. Key newspaper reports have been those by *The Hindu* and reports from the websites (IndiaTogether.com). Details of newspaper reports related to the suicides are available from the Indian Social Institute's files (Human Rights Documentation) which are available for the years 1999-2010. Reports on recent suicides in the North Indian (Orissa, West Bengal and Uttar Pradesh) belt for the period 2009-2010, are from *The Tribune*, and the websites (Orissakhabar.in). Updates from the NCRB 2010 have not been included as it was released only in October 2011.

3 Based on the excellent and comprehensive report by the organisation, Vikas Samvaad (2008) on the agricultural situation and the distress faced by agriculturists in several districts of Madhya Pradesh.

4 Details are from the excellent investigative reports completed and reported by Sudhanshu Chaudhury of Citizens News Service and available on their website (www.citizen-news.org/2008/02/chhattisgarh).

5 See article in *The Hindu* on this quote (www.hinduonnet.com/fline/fl2411/stories).

6 The NDA government, under Prime Minister Vajpayee, had constituted a National Farmers' Commission in 2004. But as they lost the parliamentary elections, a new commission under Dr. M. S. Swaminathan was constituted and the Commission delivered its report in 2006.

7 All data on the suicides from the North Indian states are from the files on agrarian suicides compiled by the Indian Social Institute (New Delhi) and available on the website (http://www.isidelhi.org.in/hrnews/HR_THEMATIC_ISSUES/Agriculture/Agriculture;pdf).

8 Data sources for the key states in which suicides have been recorded include reports by several 'fact-finding' and citizens' groups. For details on Reports commissioned and published by the Government of India see footnote number 2. Most English newspapers have provided only intermittent reports of the distress, with *The Hindu*, being an exception. Apart from writing op ed essays for *The Hindu* and periodically highlighting the complexities of the agricultural situation, P. Sainath has consistently reported on the issue in various e-magazines, including for India Together. His compilations for Andhra Pradesh, Maharashtra and Kerala form a body of material that are sensitive and representative of trends in the rural areas. Data from the National Crime Record Bureau, (NCRB) which keeps records of all crimes including suicides, is available from their website. K. Nagaraj's analysis of the NCRB data has provided a useful disaggregation of the data over regions and time. Information on Rajasthan and West Bengal were gathered from *The Tribune* and *The Telegraph*, respectively.

9 See files on farmers' suicides, Indian Social Institute, New Delhi ((http://www.isidelhi.org.in/hrnews/HR_THEMATIC_ISSUES/Agriculture/Agriculture;pdf).

10 The Karnataka Rajya Raitha Sangha (KRRS), attempting to revive its presence, has published a few reports on the issue and has, since 2006, started visiting families of agriculturists who have committed suicide and in some cases has provided compensation (communication from

Shri Veersangiah, secretary, KRRS).

11 Details are available from the website of the Mata Amritanandamayi Math (www.amritapuri.org/939/hope).

12 Details are from the *Times of India* (November 29, 2004).

13 Based on a dossier of materials sent by Shri Bharat Jhala, Gujarat.

14 Sharad Pawar, as part of the coalition government, was selected to be the Agriculture Minister in 2004 and 2009. This despite his contested record (of failing to address the problems faced by agriculturists), including allegations of corruption and promotion of only the sugarcane cultivators (as he is the chairman of the largest sugar cooperative in Maharashtra) and of spending more time on cricket (as Chair of the Board of Control of Cricket in India). His re-nomination for a second round in 2009 saw more public criticisms leveled against him.

15 From the news report, "Minister's remark sparks row in Madhya Pradesh", *The Hindu*, January 14, 2011.

16 I draw on Henri Lefebvre's (1991) concept of space to indicate the ways in which a certain area/zone/phenomena is conceived, related to, and represented.

17 I would like to thank Sowmyabrata Choudhury for pointing out to the recurring representation of agriculturists as being in a condition of pathos. I link this to the persistent denial of the structuring factors and conditions which have led to the suicides.

18 I thank Janaki Nair for highlighting this and bringing my attention to the significance of the 'Swing Riots'.

19 It is difficult to consider *sati* as a form of suicide as there is often a lack of volition on the part of the victim and many are subject to pressure and forced to perform the act as a ritual.

20 All references to the cultural and religious bases of suicide are from Thakur (1963), Elwin (1943), and Ruzika (1998). Although Thakur uses the word, *Sallekhana*, the correct term may be *Samlekhana (Sam*; praiseworthy and *Lekhana* or emasculation), or death by deliberate withdrawal from food and water, and this continues to be a way in which several Jains seek to end their lives at old age and the practice is upheld by the precepts of Jaina philosophy and is widely accepted by its

adherents (see Mody 2007).

21 Verrier Elwin's work, '*Maria Murder and Suicide*' (1943) contains great details of the conditions and personal reasons for violence among the Maria of Bastar (now in Chhattisgarh) and is an empathetic perspective on the Maria. Yet, Elwin makes no clear and explicit links between the intense colonisation of the region and the Maria society and that of seeing the forms of violence as a response to such erosion of their cultures and of the growing criminalisation of all their activities.

22 Attempts have been made to repeal the Act and to 'de-criminalise' suicides. However, there is currently a *status quo* on the Act.

23 In addition to colonial registration of suicides as illegal and anti-State acts, the government of India has initiated the suicides registries as part of the international drive to record suicides (World Heath Organisation 2000).

24 In drawing on multi-disciplinary social science approaches and perspectives, I have drawn on the disciplines of history, economics, sociology and social anthropology, and geography (critical studies) to review the vast body of data and in understanding the contexts and lives of marginalised agriculturists. Since the body of data on the agrarian suicides is vast and varied, I have sought to place emphasis on integrating both secondary and primary data by using both inductive and deductive methods, drawing on macro data and micro details about villages, groups, and individuals. For a more nuanced anthropological perspective, I have drawn on ethnographic readings of my own field notes and of case studies of families which have suffered a suicide. Although I eschew the route of postmodernism, I have drawn on Zygmunt Bauman's (2001) body of work (especially those after his critique of postmodernism) to highlight the making of 'modern' formations and the impact of such alterations on socialities and identities.

Data Analyses: In relying on secondary data sources (both official data, such as that by the National Crime Records Bureau, several government documents and data bases, and a large number of reports by NGOs and fact-finding groups, and several journalistic accounts, apart from studies), I have reviewed the validity of the data from the perspective of (a) the bases for construction of categories (2) political bases of reports and their possible biases (3) contradictions between official/ government reports versus those produced by academics and NGO reports. In reconstructing the suicides for different regions/states and for different periods, I have drawn on Charles Tilly's (2008) suggestion of undertaking 'event catalogs'. Here the 'aggregate counts' for each region and different periods, the 'incidence' account for each event, and the 'internal regularity' of these events (as reported and/or described by various authors and that of personal narratives) are analysed to form a composite and comparative picture of the event.

25 Jack Douglas' work (1966) on the study of suicide is a landmark essay on reviewing the epistemological and paradigmatic significance of Durkheim's work on suicide. As he elaborates, Durkheim's book, *Suicide,* not only provided the paradigmatic ideas about the causes of suicide (enabling them to become even commonsensical) but also established the methodology for studying social issues and rooted the ideas of 'social system' and 'social structure' as new terms which entered the common parlance in the social sciences.

26 Douglas' (1966) study questions the extension of Durkheim's categories to all situations and forms of suicides. Similarly, Bohannon's seminal study of suicide in Africa questioned the relevance of Durkheimian readings for Africa. In addition, we need to recognise that while Durkheim's contribution to sociological methods and perspectives (and in establishing the science of sociology) are central in his work, *Suicide*, his emphasis on the functional social ordering of society stands challenged (see Latour 2007) and more specifically such an organic and functionalist perspective is not valid for a society such as the caste-based Indian one.

27 See new range of suicides mentioned in the Wikipedia and in the recent studies conducted by the World Health Organisation (2000)(www.who.int/mental_health/prevention).

28 All data is sourced from the National Crime Records Bureau (2008) and from the analyses made by K. Nagaraj (2008), Sainath (2009, 2010) and the reports for each of the regions. A different reading of the data and trends is by Gruere et al. (2008) and they question the associated 'sharp' increase in suicide rates since 1997 among agriculturists and consider the NCRB data to indicate "only...a relatively minor share and stable share of total suicides in India" (2008: 5). However, I draw on the analyses by Nagaraj (2008) and Sainath (2010) and use the region-wise data of suicides by agriculturists to indicate both a sharp spurt and a growing 'epidemic of suicides' by agriculturists during this period.

29 Data for international levels of suicide are from suicide.org; an International suicide prevention group (http://www.suicide.org/international-suicide-statistics.html).

There are now three sets of powers… the party (political), the panchayat, and the local leaders. Between them they distribute what comes from the government. Nobody listens to anybody, each group is for itself.

Basavaraj Biradar, Madhbhavi Village, Karnataka, 2009

The great mass of the poor in countries are become an hereditary race, and it is next to impossible for them to get out of that state themselves.

Tom Paine, *Agrarian Justice*, 1797

Chapter Two

Ruralities and the 'Suicide Hot Spots'

> The devastation (of suicides) lies in the big five states (Maharashtra, Andhra Pradesh, Karnataka, Madhya Pradesh, and Chhattisgarh). These account for two-thirds of all suicides between 2003-2008.
> **P. Sainath, *Farm Suicides: A Twelve-year Saga*, 2010**

In what is often seen as a surprising and contradictory trend, most of the suicides have taken place in and are reported from states (Maharashtra, Karnataka, Punjab, and Andhra Pradesh) that have higher rates of economic growth and longer records of social development. Why, many have queried, have the suicides not been in the poorer states and among the poorest? More particularly, what accounts for the fact that on an average more agriculturists than non-agriculturists have committed suicides? What are the features of these regions that have rendered agriculturists so vulnerable to distress conditions? Why has rural India turned into a killing field? And why have some regions become 'suicide hotspots'?

Responses to such queries require us to better understand rural India itself. Yet, since the rural is not synonymous with the village or with the agrarian, conceptualizing and locating the suicides within the framework of rurality[1] may enable us to go beyond the typical conflation of the rural with the agrarian. Doing so may also enable us to overcome the theoretical and methodological limitations associated with studying rural and agrarian issues.[2] Some of the early sociological studies highlighted the multiple and layered linkages of villages to the larger economic, political and socio-cultural worlds,[3] and thereby contested the older, orientalist perspective of Indian villages as insular and stagnant. But over the years, as Jodhka (2005) and Thakur (2006) have highlighted, the idea and construct of the 'village' in India has become overloaded; it is either associated with idealised notions of being a repository of Indian civilisation and culture or is dismissed as an unchanging entity, which reproduces the caste system and discrimination. Recent attempts (e.g. Mines and Yazgi 2010) have sought to reclaim the epistemological and anthropological value of studying villages, and have highlighted the ways in which the village continues to be a site of symbolic and socio-political value. But, in the context of understanding the suicides, and despite nearly fourteen years since the beginning of the 'agrarian distress', there has been inadequate attention paid to the more recent complexities by which villages, regions, capital, labour, knowledge and the caste and class structures have intertwined to impact the lives of agriculturists.

Focusing on 'rurality' as a space, is to enable an integrated perspective and to shift the focus from purely administrative or government definitions which define the rural by default.[4] These definitions consider the rural as being primarily an area where agriculture is the predominant form of economic activity, have relatively low density of population, and as being diametrically opposed to the urban or city. To overcome these limitations, the concept of rurality can be "envisaged as a complex interweaving of power relations, social conventions, discursive practices and institutionalised forces which are constantly combining and recombining" (Cloke 2005:24). In doing so, one can recognise the multiplicity of factors that account for variations in rural conditions. Some of these factors are the different ecological characteristics, myriad economic activities, governance by different political and administrative apparatus, variations in linkages to towns and cities, and the manifestations of different cultural configurations. Such a definition and approach may enable us to better understand rural India in its twenty-first century moment.[5] In addition, such a perspective can also include taking into consideration factors, forms and processes of multiple 'agrarian questions'.[6]

Structuring Ruralities: Forces, Agencies, and Trends

As a key site of nation building, rural India in the immediate post-colonial phase had been subject to the agenda of political integration via the spread of political parties and electoral processes, economic development as envisaged primarily through the Green Revolution, social development primarily through the programmes of community development,[7] and specific targeted programmes such as the Integrated Rural Development Programme (IRDP). Following these and intertwined with the processes of structural adjustment and market-based economic liberalisation in the 1990s, policies and programmes of decentralised administration and the introduction of elementary education have become key aspects of governmentality in rural areas. More recently, since 2004, the intensification of neo-liberal agendas has led to the marking of the rural as an arena of new market opportunities, a space with new resources to be exploited, and yet the rural is also the site of multiple programmes of welfare governmentality, such as the National Rural Employment Guarantee Programme(NREGP) that seek to address the negative fallout of the neo-liberal economy (Sanyal 2008). Engaged in transacting and negotiating these varied economic, political-social processes, and institutions, in turn, has led to the formation and presence of a range of civil, political and moral societies[8] in the rural areas. Overarching all of these is the spread of capitalist forces, the impact of which needs to be assessed not in terms of the teleological, universal logic of capital altering structures and conditions but as also "producing effects of the contradictory dynamics of capitalist social relations – including how they reshape practices and beliefs that predate capitalism" (Brass 2010: 6). Such variations in the intermeshing of regional, social and cultural forms with political economies of change have led to subsequent differentiations in regions and to multiple forms in which they have engaged with 'modernity'. Sivaramakrishnan and Agarwal (2003) provide details of such variations and emergent forms of 'regional modernity' that break stereotypes of either submitting to the standard formats of western modernity or to being in conditions of failed modernity. Subsequently, what we have across the geo-physiographic regions and states are multiple forms of rurality which vary in their economic, political, social and cultural conditions.

Increasing Regional Differentiation

Marked by the impact of the past six decades of post-colonial, political-economic factors and varied socio-cultural patterns, we can identify at least eight distinct types of ruralities in India.[9] These range from the relatively inaccessible regions of forests and mineral wealth (typically inhabited by the Adivasi/tribal peoples) to those regions that are now integrated into the circuits of global capital and labour (such as the villages of Kerala and Punjab). In between these two extremely varied regions are the wet cultivating belts where the first Green Revolution was introduced, the dry and semi-arid regions now subjected to commercial agriculture as part of the second Green Revolution, the coastal belts, the plantation belts, the mountainous regions of the Himalayas, and the North-East. Since the mid 1990s new ruralities include belts where rural industries, including Special Economic Zones (SEZs), and new educational complexes are emerging as dominant forms of regional economy.

Each of these types of ruralities is not exclusive to any specific region or state and can instead be considered to be an enclave within states and regions. For example, the Adivasi belts which are found in states such as Madhya Pradesh, Maharashtra, and Andhra Pradesh contrast sharply with areas within the state but have commonalities with other Adivasi belts in Gujarat and Karnataka. Similarly, the new and emerging ruralities of primarily non-agricultural residential zones supported by remittance economies can be found within Punjab, Gujarat and Kerala. Variations in both 'villages' and of the types of rural areas range from those such as the relatively insular and isolated hamlets of the North-East and mountain regions, the mixed caste villages of Madhya Pradesh and Bihar and the plains in general, to the well-developed villages of Punjab and Kerala, which are now closely integrated into the circuits of international labour migration, a remittance economy, and returned diaspora. In addition, there are examples of sharp intra-state variations such as between Vidarbha (that is now recording the largest numbers of suicides by agriculturists), and Baramati (the prosperous sugarcane belt that is emerging as an agri-business-educational complex) in Maharashtra. In view of the large variations in ruralities, it is important to identify the key forces that have impacted them in the recent decades and their significance for the life conditions of those who live there.

Agricultural Modernity: The Green Revolution

Representing a form of "state-sponsored high modernist agriculture" (Scott 1998: 262), the Green Revolution is deeply implicated in the remaking of rural India with significance not only for the rural economy but also for the social structure, political patterns and ecological conditions of different ruralities. The failure of the caste-embedded agrarian structure to generate economic growth (Thorner 1972) and its low productivity became primary objects for alteration. Subsequently, the diversity and heterogeneity of agricultural forms have been subjected to the post-colonial State's agenda of systematic objectification and normalisation, which in many ways is more rigid and pervasive than the colonial objectification of India and its economy and culture. Postcolonial, state led, evaluations of different agricultural formations have been conducted with a predominant economism in which the productivity of agriculture has been privileged over all other aspects of agriculture and of rural social structure itself. Largely directed by the state and based on legitimizing compulsions of eradicating poverty, preventing famines, and boosting the nation's economic growth and self-sufficiency, India's diverse and plural agricultural formations and practices have been subject to agendas and programmes of change. Assessments of Indian agriculture as 'under developed' became a form of identity of rural India and its agriculture in the post-colonial period (Gupta 1999). Subsequently, the transformation of agriculture and agrarian communities has been based on privileging norms of productivity over ecological specificity, individual farmers' success over collective empowerment, and income growth over equitable distribution of resources.[10] This has rendered local knowledge 'archaic' (Ludden 1992), disembedded the production system from its ecological base, and initiated shifts from the local, ecological embeddedness of agriculture to a form of uniformity of agricultural practices. Buttressed by growing commercialisation of production, in several belts the growing homogenisation of agriculture is visible across the nation. The monoculture fields of wheat in the Punjab are replicated in the vast plains of Uttar Pradesh, Madhya Pradesh and north Karnataka; the fields used to cultivate commercial seeds under contract farming look similar whether they are located in Punjab or in Maharashtra; the fields growing Bt cotton are similar in Gujarat, Maharashtra, and Andhra Pradesh, and the vineyards outside Bangalore and Pune attempt to mimic the vineyards of the Mediterranean.

Thus the Green Revolution can be seen as mediating and disseminating both modernity and development. While its key objective of resolving the food crisis of the 1960s must be acknowledged, the long-term impact of this model of agriculture and its implications for reconstituting rural societies and inducing alterations in their socio-economic structures are now visible in the entrenchment of dominant, landed castes in positions of power.[11] Despite being the key source of economic modernity in rural India, the Green Revolution has not initiated any significant rupture of the existing caste-based social structure. On the contrary, several studies[12] have shown that the Green Revolution has enhanced the existing caste-based social and economic differentiation of society and has largely reproduced the caste-based structure of rural society.

The Reproduction of Caste as the Structuring Principle and Institution

As a result of the above trends, caste remains the key social structure and underlying principle that largely determines the rights and access to land and resources. It is the primary basis on which economic and political sources, institutions and networks are made available to and accessed by people. Apart from a few exceptions, where once low-ranked caste groups have become dominant castes[13] (see Jaffrelot and Kumar 2009), caste and class in the rural social and production structures and relations remain largely coterminus. While there are regional variations which are contingent on historical and economic differences and political mobilisation, there are commonalities in the ways in which differentiation/diversification of occupation are undertaken for both survival and for accumulation (Singh 2007). Based on this, we can flag some trends and conditions which mark the increasing differentiation between regions and the increasing socio-economic differentiation between the lives of various occupational and caste[14] categories of rural residents.

Upper caste groups and the predominantly established dominant castes continue to be the mainstay of economic and political matters. Members of the landed, dominant castes have been able to reap the benefits of the first round of Green Revolution agriculture and from among them a class of farmer entrepreneurs has emerged. Their economic, political and social success, which in turn has facilitated their emergence or strengthened their position as the dominant caste and as the 'proprietory classes' (Bardhan 1984), 'rich peasants', capitalist and 'progressive farmers' (Corbridge and Harriss 2000: 83), and as 'agrarian capitalist entrepreneurs' (Rutten 1995: 233) in the Green Revolution belt groups, is largely predicated on the economic gains they reaped with the Green Revolution. The surplus from their landed property is sought to be invested in the urban and trading arenas. Drawing on their caste linkages to trade and investment, it is predominantly the intermediate caste groups such as Jats in the northern belts of Uttar Pradesh, Haryana, and Rajasthan, Reddys and Kammas of Andhra Pradesh, Lingayats, Vokkaligas, and Shettys of Karnataka, Kurmis in the Madhya Pradesh and Chhattisgarh belt, the Jats and Sikhs of the north-western belts, Bhumihars of Bihar, and the Patidars of Gujarat who are now entrepreneurs with sizeable investments in the urban areas (Rutten 1995; Upadhya 1997; Jaffrelot and Kumar 2009; Rao and Reddy 2010). Access to political structures and positions have also led to gains in education and employment (Jeffrey and Lerche 2000), thereby enabling the dominant and intermediary castes to further consolidate their economic and social status. Peasant proprietory classes as the dominant castes also emerged as regional satraps capturing legislative assembly power especially in the states of Maharashtra, Karnataka and Andhra Pradesh in the South and in the Western states of Uttar Pradesh, and Rajasthan (Jaffrelot and Kumar 2009). Reddy and Mishra succinctly sum up such trends by noting that, "...by the late 1980s, the 'rich peasantry' as a class appears to have developed stakes elsewhere than agriculture. Agriculture for them served only as a political base but no longer as a source of their economic strength which came from contracts, commissions, commerce and speculative activities including real estate" (2008: 41).

The gains made by the dominant caste are in distinct contrast to that of the conditions of the middle ranking service and artisan castes for whom the Green Revolution and the intrusion of commercial products has spelt the death knell of their hereditary caste-based occupations. Weavers, potters, basket-makers, smiths, carpenters and a range of skilled persons are now without the support of either the older rural economy or that of the emerging commercial agriculture and form the largest bulk of the displaced and the migrant. Identified as 'Backward Classes' (BC) and/or as 'Other Backward Classes' (OBC), several regional groups of the intermediate castes are experiencing conditions of degradation and disadvantage that are more devastating than that of the Dalits. In regions where successful dominant caste groups have sought to deliberately move out of agriculture, the vacuum and lack of competition has encouraged some BC and OBC groups to gain entry into agriculture. Pastoral groups and non-agricultural communities such as the Banjara or Lambada in parts of Maharashtra and Andhra Pradesh are now emerging as new agriculturists. Joining the displaced artisan and service caste groups are the large pool of the small and medium cultivators (those who own less than five hectares of land), who have, in the logic of the market and without the security of institutional structures, been rendered redundant and are now largely either depeasantised, deproletarianised, dispossessed and/or displaced (Harriss 2006, Harriss-White 2003, Sanyal 2008). On the other hand, lower-ranked castes and those identified as 'Untouchables' and/or as Dalits, continue to constitute the bulk of the working and labouring poor. The inability of a range of programmes, from the Green Revolution to other development and decentralisation programmes, to challenge the caste-based structuring of agriculture and rural society in general accounts for the persistent reproduction of caste as the dominant structure that defines access to resources and to social and political position and status.

The fact that caste remains the foundational social structure and the basis of either opportunity or deprivation and disadvantage is underscored by secondary level data that indicates a strong correlation between caste and standard of living.[15] A range of revisit studies conducted in rural India[16] have consistently portrayed these trends: the consolidation of economic gains and resources by the dominant castes, the increasing differentiation between castes, the commercialisation of agricultural practices with the retention of caste-based structures of production relations, and the growing pool of the economically displaced (who are typically from lower-ranked caste groups). Economic diversification and subsequent inter-household differentiation encompass the variations in opportunities for different caste groups. Even as the upper caste and/or dominant caste groups consolidate their economic and political positions through their access to land, institutional credit, new technologies, markets, and social networks, the record for the middle and low-ranked caste groups and the working poor has been mixed.

Among themselves the middle caste agriculturists remain the most differentiated in class and range, and include those who have emerged as either 'dominant castes' or as 'capitalist farmers' within their regions or those who continue to be in conditions of landless penury (Omvedt 1992; Rao and Reddy 2010). Middle caste agriculturists, who own small parcels of land, and often combine independent cultivation (on their owned or rented land) are subject to processes of 'partial proletarianisation' in which there is "a pervasive dependence upon wage incomes, but without complete loss of control over their small plots" (Corbridge and Harriss 2000: 83) of land. While access to land, even to the smallest pieces, continues to be the aspiration of a large section of the landless, there are no assurances of guaranteed enhancement of livelihood opportunities. Conditions and processes such as lack of resources, including access to credit, degradation of land and supportive resources, especially water, and the subsequent underutilisation and non-utilisation of land have also become factors that account for the increasing pauperisation of marginal cultivators (Mishra 2010).

As sections who occupy the lowest social position, wage workers (typically also from the low-ranked caste groups) have been subject to mixed economic processes. The commercialisation of agriculture in regions where state-based support and enhanced politicisation has empowered the working poor has in some cases led to improvements in their living conditions and opportunities for the landless (as in the states of Tamil Nadu and Kerala). In areas where commercial agriculture or opportunities for employment have improved, real wages have increased and state supported provisioning of supplementary food for children, aged and lactating mothers, have stabilised their nutrition levels. But even under such conditions, where wage labour is available, the need to seek new and independent forms of social status or 'distinction' and to break away from the dominance of caste-based relations and discrimination, also accounts for the fact that many prefer to undertake agricultural work on terms such as contract and wage labour (Gidwani 2008). But for a majority of the landless, the conditions described by Jan Breman on trends in South Gujarat after nearly half a century (1968-2006) of field observations encapsulates the conditions of the working and low-ranked castes in vast regions of the nation. As Breman describes, landless labourers are largely trapped within a 'regime of poverty' which consists of "extremely uneven distribution of agrarian capital, the concentration of land-ownership among the rural minority belonging to the dominant castes, and the persistent landlessness of the bottom segments of the population" (2007: 413-414). As a result of these trends they experience increased pauperisation, reinforced by the loss of customary safety nets and the lack of replacement of such safety nets by official or formal forms of support, absence of opportunities to enhance their skills and abilities, lack of institutional support for credit, inadequate wages, poor working conditions and a continued position of social marginality. Even in cases where bonded labour is on the wane, a variation of unfree labour which Breman calls 'neo-bondage' (2007: 213) is on the rise. Low-ranked caste and tribal groups are forced, in order to provision their families or to meet social and economic expectations, to resort to submitting to landlords or owners of brick kilns, salt pans, and other contractors through 'advances', or 'loans'. These transactions keep them tied in "situations of desperate deficiency" (Breman 2007: 214) which reproduce their conditions of subordination and oppression.

Variations in economic opportunities across the caste and class groups have also initiated a range of rural economic diversification activities. Despite the vast regional and state-wise differences, some generalisations about the features of rural diversification are represented in a summary by Harriss-White's note on changes in North Arcot district in Tamil Nadu. As she sums up, there is now

> an increase in crop varieties, the introduction of perennial crops, the new crops brought under cultivation, new combinations of crops, the colonisation of wetland by dry-land crops,[17] the intensification of irrigation, electrification and mechanisation are all manifestations of agricultural diversification. The increasing range of occupations undertaken by family members and the range of types as well as scales of assets ownership is testimony enough to household diversification. The expansion of non-farm activities such as silk weaving and petty trading, transport and construction work, employment in government or in the service sector are evidence of non-agricultural diversification (2003 :117).

In summary, the working and low-ranked poor are subject to decreasing size of landholding, increase in use of family labour, indebtedness and resorting to migration and non-agricultural work to supplement their income from agriculture. In states such as Kerala and Tamil Nadu, where political mobilisation and economic opportunities have facilitated the upward mobility of once low-ranked groups, the incidence of poverty has declined over the years. Despite the fact that in some regions there are now new forms of labour contracts, employer-worker relations (Ramachandran and

Swaminathan 2005), and opportunities for improved life conditions, the overall levels of inequality continue to be marked by caste and class positions. Vakulabharanam's (2010) essay provides a succinct summary of the reproduction of inequalities among castes and classes. While the post 1990s have heralded new and higher incomes for "urban professionals (service and manufacturing), urban informal managers and owners, urban unclassified, rural moneylenders, rural professionals, absentee landlords, and rural unclassified… the biggest losers are the urban unskilled workers (both manufacturing and service), urban skilled (manufacturing) workers, rural marginal farmers and tenants, and agricultural workers" (Vakulabharanam 2010: 70). He goes on to summarise that "…the agrarian class structure itself has largely remained unchanged during the period of economic reforms even as the populous agricultural groups have witnessed relative impoverishment vis-à-vis the non-agricultural population" (2010: 73). While economic policies have largely benefited the existing upper castes, alterations in the political structures and processes have initiated new dynamics in the power structures and relations in rural India.

'Deepening Democracy' and Contested Power Regimes

The spread of democracy, primarily through the machinery and machinations of periodic elections, and the attempts to deepen it through decentralised democracy have left several imprints on India's rurality. For one, periodic elections and the backward linkages to caste groups and associations and to existing rural power structures, and the contestations over access and distribution of resources have led to the politicisation of most villages. The result has been an overall "overpoliticisation of social life in rural India" (Tanabe 2007: 561). Such politicisation is linked to the presence and impress of political parties so much so that in many regions the political party is, as in West Bengal, "…indeed the elementary institution of rural life…and mediates every single sphere of social activity, with exceptions if any" (Chatterjee 2009:43).

The decentralisation of administration via the Panchayati Raj acts and the 'deepening of democracy' through a range of localised associations and political parties, have also created a mixed and complex political situation in the rural areas. On the one hand, decentralisation (where implemented) has facilitated the social legitimacy of low-ranked caste groups to become political actors and in generating a sense of possible change and empowerment among the masses. On the other hand, in most rural areas and regions, low-ranked caste groups remain either proxy candidates or captive members of political parties within the continued leadership hold of the upper and dominant caste members. Further, drawing from the caste-based patron-client system,[18] the *jajmani* system continues to be the model in which most political parties function, and the processes and practices of genuine democratic structures are largely absent. Yet, such intense politicisation of rural societies has not assured benefits of political mobilisation to the most disadvantaged. Dalits and Adivasis are yet to gain as is increasingly evident from the recent mobilisation against the state by Adivasis in the new, predominantly Adivasi states of Jharkhand and Chhattisgarh. In addition, the capture of the State and its machinery, including the promotion of unfettered capital and market interests, by elite groups have compromised the possibility of inclusive development.

But, as much as such decentralised administration is also associated with attempts and policies to deepen democracy, the implication of such decentralisation must also be factored. In fact Mahmood Mamdani's (2001) observation about colonial Africa that the departments for 'local government' were really departments for the control and capture of peasants is largely true for rural India as well. Governmental reach into the realms of village, community, and family has been deployed through various agencies such as the departments of agriculture, community development, health, and elementary education. But such governmental and democratic reach has not necessarily led to improvement in the conditions of life of the vast majority (Vakulabharanam 2010) and the low development indices in many areas are evidence of this. Deepening democracy is also matched with an increase in the number of middle men and agents who as power brokers and 'political entrepreneurs' (Krishna 2003: 1174) mediate between the large body of rural residents and the various agencies of the State. The result is the spread of various forms of illegalities in which the poor and disadvantaged are caught including the new forms of bondage to leaders as they seek their assistance and patronage to either receive welfare goods and services, or seek redressal from the larger system (Chatterjee 2009). Other trends which have impacted the fabric of ruralities relate to the patterns of migration and to the subsequent change in land use, household, and labour use patterns.

Mobilities and Migration

Regions which are generally marked by low development, and by the lack of availability of work and/or access to land for the landless, are witness to migration as a form of livelihood option.[19] Although inter-regional and rural-urban migration has not increased since the 1980s, Kundu (2006) has observed that such migration is not primarily from the rural to the urban areas and is instead circular in which rural residents move seasonally in search of work and return to their home base periodically. Further, given the sharp regional variations, labour-linked migration is also intra-regional, with labour pools moving from region to region depending on the availability of work. New trends indicate the movement of both workers seeking employment in sites other than their place of origin and that of agricultural entrepreneurs who seek new lands and resources to expand their growing capital. Matching these complex trends in migration, and the subsequent alterations in the constitution of households and villages, are policies and programmes that have resulted in large scale displacement of populations from rural belts. 'Development' related activities, such as construction of dams, mining, electricity generation, establishment of large scale public sector factories etc., account for between 50-60 million being displaced without rehabilitation or relocation (Fernandes 2008). Among the displaced population, a significant proportion (upto 40 per cent) are Adivasis or tribals and another 20 per cent are Dalits (Fernandes 2008).

Feminisation of Agriculture

The disembedding rural economy, which sees large numbers of the indigent and the impoverished migrate to external sites of work, also skews the gender-based allocation of agricultural work. This results in, especially in the high growth regions and in the poor, dryland areas with high male out-migration belts, feminisation of agriculture (Vepa 2009; Garikipati 2009). Women are either integrated into agricultural wage labour or become by default the *de facto* cultivators of land, even though in most cases they are not entitled to ownership of land.[20] Between 1961 and 2001, the proportion of women agricultural labourers increased from 25.6 per cent to 43. 4 per cent (Garikipati 2009). Forming a total of 46.9 per cent of the total agricultural labour force, women are increasingly the key workers in a variety of agricultural tasks and responsibilities. In the 150 poorest districts of the nation, there are now more women agricultural labourers than male (Krishnaraj and Kanchi 2008), a situation that highlights the growing distress in these regions. The implications of this are multiple. As men eke out lives as migrant workers on construction sites, in urban and semi-urban industrial areas, as service workers and as agricultural workers in other regions or districts, the village has been relegated to becoming sites of reproduction. Households, run by women, who in turn become primarily responsible for the family and dependents (both the elderly and the young), have become the norm in several regions and account for the increasing feminisation of poverty (Krishnaraj and Kanchi 2008; Vepa 2009). At the same time, there is no clear evidence if the increased decision-making roles also enable a more autonomous or empowered position for women. A reverse trend of the integration of women from the high migration belts into the lower ranks of the service economy and varied industrial units can be seen in the growing numbers of women who migrate out as domestic servants (and as allied service providers or as low-ranked industrial workers) into urban and semi-urban areas and who become the key sources of income for their families. The growing pool of Adivasi/tribal women as domestic workers in urban areas also represents this trend.

In summary, the making of rural India and its ruralities has been marked by varied factors and forces. Democracy and development agendas that form the basis of governmentality,[21] the Green Revolution as the key paradigm of economic growth, and the more recent intrusion of capital, the market and media have significance for the structuring of rural India. All of these are qualified by the very social and economic position (caste and class) of different groups and have become the bases for varied degrees of social and economic aspirations and account for the myriad ways in which large numbers of people are seeking to alter their life-worlds and status. Much of these are then translated into the larger canvas of regions and the result is visible in the emergent new ruralities that represent sharply contradictory trends and tensions. In the retention of caste as a structuring principle and organisation lies the coinciding of economic and social power; the promotion and spread of electoral democracy and decentralised administration has led to some shifts in the source of political power; customary culture, with its apparatus of rituals and practices has met with consumer culture (abetted by the spread of media) to make for an enhanced density of rituals embellished with an assortment of goods; local knowledge systems stand to be erased, as knowledge from and of the external world make inroads into shaping livelihoods. Even as land as the site of agricultural practice has become a source of contention, land as a source of identity "which has commanded great affective power" (Datta 2008: 18) continues to be associated with a sense of belonging. For lower-ranked caste groups, and those typically considered marginal to and outside the core of agricultural landholding, the ability to access land and to engage with new agriculture forms a source of new identity and a way out of a life of economic and social marginality. Buttressing much of this are trends where education is sought by many as a source of opportunity and a marker of new and altered status and a form of distinction. As capital makes inroads into the economic and social lives of people, it creates new opportunities and burdens, marking people as either creditors or debtors. Labour circulates back and forth from villages to other villages and to towns and cities in conditions not completely as 'free wage labour' but as a source of cheap labour tied in various forms to social structures of exploitation. Shifts, in some regions, such as the growth of non-agricultural villages, in which either the remittance economy or incomes from a range of non-agricultural sources have gained prominence (Gupta 2004; Nayyar and Sharma 2005) do not significantly alter the very foundational bases of rural India. A range of forms of governmentality seeks to act as the agency of modernity, democracy, and equity, bringing with it new aspirations and re-aligning social relations and obligations.

Linked to the immediate worlds of regional economies, or to larger networks of migration, remittance economy, and to circuits of capital and labour, villages form parts of varied ruralities. In these interlinks and despite the tremendous variations in ruralities, the village continues to be the epicentre where "pushes from villages form extensions, expansions, and even expulsions of different practices and people. Villages mediate and structure these pushes, such that different people are differently exposed and vulnerable" (Schlesinger 2010: 228). And it is in the making of these regional variations and life-conditions of people, including the differences in the forms and levels of vulnerabilities, that will enable us to delineate the features of the ruralities which emerged as what were popularly referred to as the 'suicide hotspots'.

The Making of the 'Suicide Hotspots'

The political economy of the state, the economic and social structures of regional agricultures, the role of the market, market agencies, and capital account for significant differences in the manifestations of distress conditions and the spread of suicides by agriculturists. Vidarbha, Marathwada, and Khandesh in Maharashtra, Telangana, Rayalaseema, and north coastal districts in Andhra Pradesh, the Malwa belt in Punjab, and the hill districts of Wayanad and Idukki in Kerala have emerged as 'suicide hotspots' since 1997. Only in Karnataka were suicides reported from across the state and were not restricted to any specific district or region. Although there are some differences between the regions, there are underlying similarities between them which also account for the commonalities in the contexts and reasons for the victims to have committed suicide.

For one, most of the affected regions (Vidarbha, Marathwada, Khandesh, Telangana, Rayalaseema, North coastal Andhra, North Karnataka, and the Malwa belt) are ecologically fragile regions with large stretches of semi-arid tracts and have development indices[22] that are lower than the average in each of their respective states. Although Idukki and Wayanad are mountainous regions with rich biodiversity, both the districts are also considered to be relatively 'backward' (Nair and Menon 2009) in comparison to other districts in Kerala. The period of the mid 1980s onwards witnessed the integration of these regions into the dominant development model of the states. High prices for each of the agricultural commodities during the 1980s, and peaking during the early 1990s, accounted for the fact that several marginal cultivators also sought to be integrated into this model. That the ecological and economic conditions had altered by the late 1990s, and were now manifesting as distress conditions is largely reflective of the impact of such economic models on them.

All the states, Punjab, Maharashtra, Karnataka, and Andhra Pradesh reporting high levels of suicide by agriculturists, have been keen promoters of economic liberalisation in general, including that in agriculture (Bhalla and Singh 2009). Economic policies in these states have over the period, particularly since 1993, privileged urban over the rural economies, and have facilitated the intrusion of capital and commercial enterprises into the rural belts. Private capital investment in these states have been above the national average (Reddy and Mishra 2008), and several policies have been deployed to facilitate shifts in land-use and the development of a 'vibrant land market' to match the new regime of neo-liberal industrialisation and infrastructure development. Attendant with these policies has been the underinvestment in public infrastructure such as irrigation, water management, and research (Vaidyanathan 2006). Policies such as these have meant that far from recognizing the ecological specificities of each of these regions, they have been integrated into the dominant economic and agricultural model.

State policies and programmes in each of these states have also focused on shifting from "low-value food grains to high-value non-foodgrain crops" (Bhalla and Singh 2009: 36). Regions which had for long cultivated coarse foodgrains (millets and pulses) witnessed shifts in cultivation to commercial crops of groundnut, cotton and tobacco in the dry districts and to crops like rice and vegetables in the wet districts. In North Karnataka, Bidar district, once known for its cultivation of millets, agriculturists shifted since the late 1980s to the production of *tur* (red gram). In the southern districts of Karnataka, such as in Hassan, Mandya, and Davangere, where improvements in irrigation had generated shifts to wet cultivation, agriculturists took to the production of vegetables for the market. In Punjab, in the Malwa region, otherwise a dry tract with a fragile ecology, the Green Revolution package with its focus on wheat and rice production, led to increased use of water, technology (tube-wells, tractors, tillers, harvesters etc.) and capital. Wayanad and Idukki districts in Kerala recorded an increase in plantation cash crops (from 16 per cent in 1990-93 to 36 per cent in 2003-06 [Nair and Menon 2009]) of spices (cardamom, pepper etc.) and a sudden spurt in the growing of vanilla.

In the Vidarbha region, the semi-arid belts of the districts of Akola, Washim, and Amaravathi, and the central Vidarbha districts of Wardha and Yavatmal, which have recorded the nation's largest numbers of suicides, have also been subject to substantial alteration of their agriculture. Shifting from mixed cultivation of millets and pulses, the commercial cultivation of sorghum, pearl millet, red gram, and cotton in the semi-arid belts and paddy, red chillies, sorghum, soya, and cotton in the central districts have gained prominence. In the Marathwada districts of Beed and Parbhani which also recorded suicides, agriculturists had taken to cultivating cotton and soya in addition to the staple crops of sorghum and some pulses.

Each of these regions has also recorded higher than national averages in the use of commercial agricultural inputs (Bhalla and Singh 2009). Andhra Pradesh and the affected districts that have recorded high levels of suicide also report the nation's highest proportion of pesticide usage (Galab et al. 2009). Punjab retains its position in the production and sales of agricultural implements (with every third farming family owning a tractor [Singh 2007]) and with levels of expenditure on agricultural inputs such as pump sets being one of the highest in the country. Each of these regions also recorded higher costs of cultivation than the other regions within the states and in comparison to other states (Bhalla 2006).

Data on rural indebtedness indicates that most of the affected states also recorded higher than national average levels of indebtedness. The proportion of indebted agriculturists for Andhra Pradesh, Punjab, Kerala and Karnataka was 82, 65, 64 and 62 per cent respectively (NSSO 2005). The amount of debts in each of these regions was also higher than the other states, with Punjab recording the highest amount, followed by Andhra Pradesh, and Kerala. Each of these regions also recorded an increase in the presence and numbers of moneylenders, including the growth of agribusiness agents and traders acting as new agricultural lenders. Interlinked markets, where agencies and agents are the source of credit, sale of agricultural inputs, and buyers of agricultural produce, have also increased in these regions.

The growth of private money lenders in these regions has also become one of the key factors (Reddy and Mishra 2008; Bhalla and Singh 2009; Vakulabharanam 2010). As states where capital growth and flows were encouraged, and availability of credit from institutional sources dried up, it was the private moneylender who gained entry and presence among marginal cultivators who otherwise lacked the wherewithal to access low-interest credit. Subsequently, these regions have manifested what has been identified as 'distress inducing growth' (Vakulabharanam 2009), where interlinked markets and growing production costs trap agriculturists into ever increasing cycles of debt and production (more details in Chapter III).

A key sociological factor, that distinguishes these states from the others that did not record suicides, relates to the relative shifts in the agrarian social structures and economic mobilities of the various caste groups. In Andhra Pradesh, the Telangana region, which recorded the highest number of agriculture related suicides, had witnessed interesting trends in land holding and cultivation patterns. Although cotton cultivation had been introduced into the region since the turn of the 20th century, the past two decades (since late 1980s) had witnessed substantial changes in agricultural patterns and in the agrarian social structure (Venkateshwarlu 1998). Once a region where a small minority of persons owned large landholdings, while a large mass of landless workers cultivated the lands, it had changed to intense cultivation of commercial crops by migrant landowners from the coastal belts of the state. While cotton and commercial cultivation of red gram, green gram and groundnut had gained momentum, the successful landed elite had moved away from cultivation as they sought better economic opportunities in the cities and towns and the growing presence of naxalites had become a threat to their continued hold over large landholdings (Venkateshwarlu 1998). A result of such trends meant that while tenancy had increased, the average size of the holding had decreased. A significant proportion of such cultivators were also 'Backward Caste' members. Similarly, in Maharashtra, the dry belts of the Vidarbha had seen changes in rural occupational structures, with more of the 'Backward Castes' (otherwise associated with service skills) taking to agriculture (Mohanty 2005). Although Punjab records an increase in the consolidation of landholdings by the rich and a growing pauperisation of marginal cultivators, the existing marginal cultivators have also sought to be integrated into the dominant model of agricultural production.

Even as successful dominant castes, who have been both the pioneers and the beneficiaries of the Green Revolution, have sought to move out of agriculture, the vacuum created in the agricultural economy and facilitated by regional forms of caste mobility have enabled members of the 'Backward Castes' to become full-time cultivators. In addition, many of them, typically non-cultivating castes, have also sought to emulate the Green Revolution or commercial agricultural practices of the local dominant castes. This largely draws from the fact that in each of the regions, Andhra Pradesh's Kammas, Kapus and Reddys, the Marathas in Maharashtra, the Jat Sikhs in Punjab, and the Vokkaligas and Lingayats of Karnataka have become the model for widespread emulation and social mimicry by other subordinate castes. In seeking to follow them, there has been the spread of the Green Revolution model not only as a form of agricultural practice but also as a form of modernity and social mobility. Additional benefits from the Green Revolution, which include political possibilities and non-agricultural gains, have only further made the Green Revolution and commercial agriculture more attractive to all sections of rural society.

Each of the regions has manifested a coming together of triple crises; economic, social and ecological. While the economic crises have been in the form of decreasing land availability and the increasing costs of cultivation along with the higher risks of production and sales, the social crises are manifested at the level of increasing vulnerability of marginal agriculturists. All agriculturists are also subject to the intensification of resource depletion which includes the decreasing fertility of soil, the decline of the water table, and loss of biodiversity.

The making of these regions into high vulnerability or 'suicide hotspots' calls attention to some of the complexities in the emergent forms of rurality. Most of the suicide belts have been relatively fragile ecological regions, which have been integrated into commercial agriculture only in the past two decades. They have experienced shifts in the agrarian social structure with small cultivators taking to commercial agriculture. Volatile (for prices of commodities) and unregulated (for lack of assurance of quality in agricultural inputs) markets combined with the burden of capital intensive cultivation have laid the foundations of rendering these cultivators and regions into 'suicide hotspots'. In the altered societies, economies and ecologies, within which small and marginalised cultivators seek new economic enterprises and social mobility, lies the very contradictions of these emergent ruralities. Those very structures (state support and stable markets) that were enabling for a previous generation of cultivators are both unavailable and unpredictable for the new and marginal cultivators. Hence, what we have in the remaking of India's rurality are the entry of marginalised cultivators into models of commercial agricultural production which are no longer sustainable of the household economy, the local ecological conditions, and the cultivator themselves.

While the State, capital, and market either alter or consolidate the structures of class positions, labour, knowledge and identities, the caste system has become the key basis for cultural and political mobilisation. The import of this is that while rural India remains structurally unaltered, in as much as caste remains the structuring principle and organisation which determines privileges and deprivations, it is also significantly changed. The nature of agricultural production, the types of crops, the linkages to market and capital, and the role of government agencies and the new political apparatus have made such changes possible. While class power and privilege have largely consolidated at the upper caste-class levels and have lent themselves to the transformations of these groups into urban and even global economic players, the forms of deprivation and disarray have intensified at the lower caste-class levels. Caught in between these are a number of middle caste and class groups for whom the dominant model of economic growth and socio-cultural aspirations remains that of the dominant castes and their engagement with commercial models of agricultural production. Details of the impact of commercial agriculture and its implications for the life-worlds of the majority of cultivators, the marginalised agriculturists, will throw light on the ways in which the existing structure of agriculture and the enveloping of most agriculturists in a web of risks lay the foundation for making agriculture, long known as a gamble in the monsoon, to become even more risk-laden.

Notes

1 The term rurality, in sociological literature, has been used primarily to refer to the growth of non-urban areas and zones in the post-industrial West, where the rural is no longer primarily the agrarian but incorporates economies of tourism and residential areas and is also the site where agendas related to biodiversity and new renewable sources of energy are sited (Cloke 2006). But as Cloke argues, the term has the potential to capture and represent key characteristics of varied rural formations including that of their functions, their political economies and their cultural specificities. Veiga (2004) and Dalla Costa (2007) consider the validity of the term for even non-Western countries and indicate this to be a way to capture the altering political economies and continued interlinks between the urban and the rural.

2 Until recently most studies have segregated the study of rural areas into specialised bodies of knowledge much of which has led to atomizing various aspects of the rural. 'Village studies' focus on the sociological aspects of villages or on their internal ordering and functioning, 'agrarian studies' have focused on a range of issues relating to practices and trends in agrarian structures and processes, and 'peasant studies' seek to understand the identity, roles, and actions of agriculturists constructed primarily as 'peasants'. In addition to these, details of rural areas, of the conditions of peasants and the debates related to development, change, forms of movements etc., have been spread across a number of disciplines including that of 'development studies' and with those that address environmental and ecological issues under 'environmental studies'.

3 A large body of literature including debates between Louis Dumont and M.N. Srinivas focus on the sociological reality of caste versus that of the village.

4 The office of the Census of India defines the rural only by default, that is, it identifies characteristics of the urban (areas with a population of more than five thousand persons; with more than seventy five per cent in non-agricultural occupations, and with a population density of more than four hundred persons per square kilometre) and the rest is assumed to be rural (censusindia.gov.in/Metadata/Metada.html).

5 The relevance and contextualisation of the term rurality, for India, as an encompassing concept are not elaborated here. Work on the idea and the

details of the various ruralities (at least eight types) is currently under progress.

6 For details of discussions on the new agrarian questions see the volume edited by Akram-Lodhi and Christobal Kay (2009).

7 I do not elaborate on the Community Development programme as it was limited to certain areas and also failed to generate any substantial changes in rural India. The Integrated Agricultural Development Programme (IADP) has been more durable and widespread but its impact has been questionable and varied; see Shah et al. (2007) for more details.

8 Tanabe (2007) contextualises his description of a 'post, post colonial society' by drawing on the definitions of civil society as that which mediates between the family and the State, political society (as defined by Partha Chatterjee) as associations formed by the poor and disenfranchised (as population) who seek to garner or demand benefits from the State, and a moral society as one in which people draw on practical-moral relationships to negotiate in the wider socio-political world.

9 The eight types of ruralities are: (1) Remote Adivasi inhabited areas (2) Agro-forestry-pastoral and mountainous belts (Himalayan tracts); (3) North-East horticulture cum forestry belts (4) Plantation belts (5) Plains; Green Revolution Phase I; wet-cultivation (6) Plains; semi-arid, Green Revolution Phase II (7) Coastal; fishing and trading and agricultural belts (8) Predominantly non-agricultural, rural belts (both remittance economy and settlements outside large industrial belts).

10 See Akhil Gupta (1998).

11 It would be inadequate to assess the Green Revolution as a single phase project. Instead, it can be assessed in terms of its three phases; namely, the initial period (1962-63 to 1980-83); the Maturing Period (1980-83 to 1990-93) and the Liberalisation Period (1990-93 to 2003-06); see Bhalla and Singh 2009.

12 Key studies of the Green Revolution in different regions of India have been those by Omvedt (1992); Shiva (1991) and several others. The one by Shiva (1991) highlights the ecological, economic and political fall-out, and more recently Sukhpal Singh (2004) has discussed the lack of sustainability of the Green Revolution model in Punjab. Other

studies such as that by Revathi and Murthy (2005) call attention to the compounding of problems in the context of the neo-liberal economic policies. For more recent reviews of the conditions in the Punjab see Gill (1995), Gill and Singh (2006) and also Newman (2007).

13 Cases of low-ranked castes becoming dominant castes have been recorded for only some areas and include belts in Tamil Nadu and Kerala.

14 I have deliberately identified occupation and caste as key categories and not that of class as the definition and identification of groups by class is contentious. Since caste and class coincide in a large majority of cases, the specificities of each of the categories or groups of people is well represented.

15 See the study by Satish Deshpande (2003) that relies on data from the National Sample Survey (NSSO 2000) and highlights the near coinciding of caste status with standards of living; with upper castes having higher incomes and standards of living and consumption and the reverse holding true for lower-ranked castes. Vakulabharanam's study (2010) on inequality seconds much of the findings of the growing inequality between classes in the rural areas.

16 There have been a number of revisit studies of village and agrarian India, but the most significant ones have been the following: Gilbert Slater's 1918 studies of villages in Tamil Nadu have been restudied by MIDS, Chennai, and John Harriss et al. (2010). A near continuous study (including intensive ethnographic work) has been done in Rampur, the village first studied by the Wisers in the 1920s and subsequently followed up by Susan Wadley in Uttar Pradesh. Scarlett Epstein's study (2003) of two villages in Mandya district, Karnataka range from the years 1954-62 and then restudied in 1970 and 1996. Studies by V. K. Ramachandran (see Ramachandran and Swaminathan 2005) and Venkatesh Athreya et al. and studies by Barbara Harriss-White and S. Janakarajan (2004) represent those for Tamil Nadu and provide excellent diachronic portrayals and highlight new trends and issues. A good summary of other revisit studies for South India is available in Rao and Nair (2003). John Harriss et al. (2010) raise pertinent issues in his summary and update on rural studies. The ICRISAT panel data for some select villages in Andhra Pradesh and Maharashtra have been analysed and presented by Rao and Nair (2003). For Gujarat, one of the earliest studies, that by J.C. Kumarappa in 1929 for Matar Taluka, has been re-visited in 1965-66 by the Planning Commission and then again

by Gidwani (2008). Although all the studies use varied indicators and do not follow a single format, the key factors of land use, ownership, labour, income and land relations can be assessed from these studies and the changes followed. For an excellent update on revisit studies in Andhra Pradesh see Rao and Reddy (2010).

17 This needs to be clarified as in most cases it is the production of wet-land crops in dry areas (using irrigation facilities) that is a key feature of the new agricultural practices.

18 The patron-client system is typically referred to as the *jajmani* system in North India and as the *balutedar* system in Maharashtra and was a form of rural economy in which there was inter-generational ties of work and social obligations between landed families as patrons and the service and labouring castes as the clients. The system has also been studied as a form of rural moral economy (see Vasavi 1999).

19 Out migration in the developed regions include that in Punjab and Kerala and are a combination of push and pull factors and are associated with strong diaspora links. Here the focus is on the inter-regional migration primarily for livelihoods.

20 Recent national level legal promulgations insist on the recognition of women's rights to land and to property but the cultural and familial resistance to such equal rights to property are yet to be addressed.

21 By governmentality I refer to the processes and structures by which the lives (biological, social, political, and economic) of people are supervised and altered and the idea is drawn from Foucault's concept of governmentality. The idea is further developed in the last chapter and is linked to Sanyal's (2008) discussion of 'welfare governmentality'.

22 For details of development indices for each of the affected districts see the Development Reports for each of the states.

I grew *tur* (red gram) as the prices were good...but the market seeds produced pests in the fields, and the sprays did not curb them. We did not eat the *tur*... the pests ate us.

Shivanna, agriculturist, Bidar district, 1999

...the risk regime is a function of a new order, it is not national, but global.

Ulrich Beck, *World Risk Society*, 1999

Chapter Three

Agriculture and the Web of Risks

> In the second phase (of the Green Revolution) expansion of commercial crops like cotton and chillies among small holdings in a situation of meager physical and financial resources and the intermittent fluctuations in crop yields, super imposed exploitative input and output linked markets (and) have highly destabilised the small farm economy culminating in large scale suicides.
>
> **Citizens' Report, 1998**

Details from the various reports[1] for the states (Maharashtra, Andhra Pradesh, Karnataka, Kerala, Punjab), in which suicides by agriculturists were studied or reported, indicate several commonalities in agricultural practices, the links between the market and agriculturists, and in the overall conditions of agriculturists in the affected regions. A feature that stands out is the fact that most of the victims were undertaking cultivation of crops primarily for the market. In the districts of Warangal and Guntur in Andhra Pradesh many of the victims were cultivating commercial crops such as cotton (Citizen's Report 1998; Prasad 2003) as were those in Maharashtra's Yavatmal and Amravati districts (Mohanty 2005). The TISS report (Dandekar et al. 2005) for the Vidarbha, Marathwada and Khandesh regions indicates that seventy per cent of the cultivators were cotton growers, while five per cent had crops under horticulture and another twenty per cent cultivated red gram, soyabean, vegetables and sugarcane. In Kerala's Wayanad belt, where a number of suicides were reported, agriculturists were entering into the export market by growing plantation crops of pepper, coffee, and vanilla (Mohanakumar and Sharma 2005). In the districts of Belgaum and Gulbarga in Karnataka, victims were growing sugarcane (Government of Karnataka 2002).

Drawing on secondary and household data for three districts (Washim, Yavatmal and Wardha) of Maharashtra, Mishra (2006) details the increase in cotton, sugarcane and oilseeds cultivation while recording the sharp decline in cereal production in the region. Groundnut had become a dominant crop in Andhra Pradesh's Anantpur district (Citizens' Report 1998). In Punjab, it was primarily the commercially oriented 'wheat and rice combination' (IDC 1998, Iyer and Manick 2000). An exception to the predominance of commercial crops is reported for Karnataka by the Expert Committee which notes that "low value, low yield cereals predominate the cropping pattern of the households" (Government of Karnataka 2002: 44) in which suicides took place. Other studies, however, note the cultivation of new and commercial crops such as potatoes, sugarcane, lentils, and vegetables in many of the districts which reported suicides (Vasavi 1999; Shivaramaiah 2007).

This commonality across the regions, where commercial agriculture had gained prominence and/or where marginal cultivators were attempting to enter into commercial agriculture, holds the key to understanding the complexities and pressures that the agriculturists in these regions, especially marginal cultivators, faced. The picture that emerges from the range of case studies across the affected states is that of the impact of commercialised agriculture, based primarily on the Green Revolution model, which then posed risks to the livelihoods and lives of agriculturists. The pattern of cultivation, the crops grown, the 'process of production' (Amin 1982),[2] the economic and social status of the victims, and the range of risks borne by them highlight the ways in which the Green Revolution marks their economic and social lives. Focusing on these factors and processes will enable us to discern the web of risks and the key obstacles and hurdles that most agriculturists face.

Remaking Agriculture

Although neo-liberal economic policies have marked the national economy since 1991, its application to the agricultural sector has not followed international trends where there has been a significant "focus on export agriculture at the cost of the domestic market" (Akram-Lodhi 2010: 270). Yet, changes in orientation, partial removal of state support, and the promotion of the market have led to "rising income and regional disparities, deceleration in the reduction of poverty, and rural distress embedded in agrarian crisis" (Reddy and Mishra: 2009: 3). Given this complexity, it may be pertinent to see how the existing and entrenched structures and conditions of India's rurality and agrarian society have compounded the situation of increasing class differentiation and the impoverishment of marginal cultivators. To emphasise these extra-economic factors is to highlight how neo-liberalism is not a universalist narrative or agenda that acts uniformly across the world. Instead, as Kingfisher and Muskovsky (2008) have pointed out, it is central that we see how neo-liberalism is a process which lends itself to localisation by interacting in varied ways with different cultural and political formations and, in many contexts and situations, it strengthens the existing structures of inequity rather than generating any substantial transformation.

In the context of it being deployed in the rural and agrarian contexts of India, neo-liberalism has been implemented gradually and policies have varied in different domains in the agricultural sector. An assessment of the impact of neo-liberalism in agriculture and the rural sector needs to factor the changes in policies relating to the agrarian economy and rural India, the role of the State, the linkages between agriculturists, the market and the State, and the overall impact of this on the most vulnerable sections of the rural population.[3] Pre-1991 economic plans, including the five-year plans and the range of development programmes, sought to address issues of equity, land distribution, and the overall problems of poverty and growing population. Subsequently, policies and a plethora of programmes focused, even if restricted to only parts of the country, on "public investments in infrastructure, irrigation, institutional financing, transport, storage and marketing" (Rao and Reddy 2010: 27). The earlier phase, especially from 1967 and up to the late 1980s, of promoting the Green Revolution model entailed significant State support in the form of capital availability, establishment of farmer training centres, subsidies for fertilisers, seeds and technology, and a remunerative price regime (Vyas 2004; Bhalla and Singh 2009; Rao and Reddy 2010). The induction of the neo-liberal economic programme since 1991 has emphasised the withdrawal of State support and subsidies from agriculture as a primary and stated goal. However, in reality the State has been cautious. Input subsidies for fertilisers, power, and irrigation have largely remained intact (Aggarwal 2006) and have primarily benefited either the fertiliser and pesticide industries or large farmers especially those in the northern and central wheat belts and in the sugarcane and commercial crop belts of Maharashtra. Policies and discussions related to minimum support prices for major crops have vacillated from possible withdrawal to its continuation, primarily out of fear of political retaliation (Guruswamy et al. 2008). But the key areas of withdrawal of the State have been in the budgetary allocation for the agricultural sector, which has witnessed successive decline. From a share of 14 per cent of budgetary allocation during the First Plan (1951-56), there has been a drastic reduction since the Sixth Plan (1980-85) to 5.8 per cent and a further reduction since 1997 to 4.9 per cent during the Ninth Plan (1997-2002) period. Average state level expenditure on agricultural infrastructure has also declined since 1997 and was only 5 per cent of the average state allocations during the year 2001-02 (Bhalla 2006). In terms of institutional changes, the neo-liberal phase has meant a withdrawal from any commitment to land reform and resource distribution. In addition, a focus on promoting increased productivity through new technologies and access to larger markets, including that of opening up to imports from international markets has been the recent policy thrust of the government. Across regions and stipulated in various state policies and abetted by a range of programmes and decisions is the focus on "...creating (value-additions) in agriculture, consolidation of land holdings by changing lease structures, and investment of corporate capital in agriculture" (Vakulabharanam 2005: 974-975).

This emphasis on facilitating agricultural productivity so as to lead to economic growth, has also meant laying stress on the efficiency of individual farmers, competitiveness among all industries, and policies that envisage and endorse a shift of the rural population towards the urban sectors. In addition, policy statements repose faith in the ability of the new technologies which are to be deployed into the rural and agricultural domain with the expectations that new communication technologies would enable and expedite agriculturists' access to new knowledge, know-how and to the market (Kumar 2009). Subsequent to such policies, both public and private investment in agriculture have declined and have led to "a collapse of agricultural infrastructure, shrinkage of credit flows, slackening of agricultural research and extension, and lack of development of new marketing and other institutions to revitalise agriculture to withstand global competition" (Bhaumik 2008: xiv).

These shifts in policies have combined with local structures of agriculture and conditions of production to induce a web of risks that have intensified pre-existing uncertainties and are largely responsible for making agriculture an unviable livelihood, that many seek to leave. As studies by various scholars[4] have elaborated, the initiation of neo-liberal fiscal policies has meant a significant drying up of institutional finance available for agriculture and rural areas in general, a decline in government expenditure on infrastructure including that for the vital irrigation sector, and a visible decrease in the presence of the state-based agricultural extension service which had been providing important information and knowledge support to agriculturists (Vyas 2004; Bhalla 2006). But, contrary to widespread assertions, the neo-liberal regime and the subsequent trade liberalisation has not directly and/or adversely affected prices of most crops and it is only the fibres, oilseeds, and plantation crops that have been subject to sharp fluctuations (see Balakrishnan et al. 2008; Radhakrishna Committee, GoI 2007). The access to markets and the promotion of cultivation of new and non-food crops have led to a decline in the area under food crops and to a visible shift to non-food crops (Bhalla and Singh 2009).

The new forms of cultivation are now seen as the model through which both individual growth and prosperity and the collective goals of rural development and agricultural growth are to be attained. Even as the agricultural extension service, with its network of agricultural agents and motivators, has declined, the growing dependence on commercial agricultural inputs has led to the growth of the presence of agents of various national and international agri-business companies in the agricultural belts where commercial agriculture is being promoted. As many of the reports on the suicides from the various states highlight, in many districts and villages it is the agents of the agri-business companies whose presence and influence is more marked than that of the State's extension workers.

Deregulation of the banking sector has meant the drying up of funds to the rural and cooperative sectors, thereby enhancing a credit squeeze (Ramachandran and Swaminathan 2005; Sriram 2008; Shah et al. 2007) even as the promoted model of Green Revolution agriculture requires more external inputs and therefore more credit. Despite variations in regional state agricultural policies[5] there are now commonalities across the nation. The new market-oriented agricultural regime, building on the establishment of the Green Revolution, is promoted through a parade of capital, technology, and new inputs to agriculturists for whom these stand as routes to a new future, a marked shift from the life of privation of their ancestors. Images of bountiful crops, miraculous technologies, easy credit, new seeds, crops and cultivation techniques bombard the average agriculturist through hoardings, television advertisements and radio jingles. Such an agenda also coincides with the promotion of the second phase[6] of the Green Revolution, as the signature programme of agricultural modernity, to enter the semi-arid and dry regions and co-opt marginal and small agriculturists into its regime.[7] As Aggarwal (2006) astutely points out, while the first phase of the Green Revolution focused only on agriculturists who had access to resources (land, capital and irrigation), the spread of commercial agriculture in this phase of globalisation has enveloped even the marginal and small cultivators. The result has been that agricultural undertakings, especially those by marginal cultivators (that were attempts to engage with the market, gain profits, and break out of the cycle of poverty and deprivation) have become the most vulnerable. Testimonials from families of victims highlight this.

Narayanamma, widow of Thimmanna of Chinnampalli village in Andhra Pradesh, said that her husband borrowed money and got bore-wells dug at six places in their eight acres of land but all of them failed. While the debt-burden of their family was increasing on the one hand, the crops had been failing for the past three years on the other, making their lives miserable. Meanwhile the bankers and landlords put pressure on her husband to clear his debts. Unable to bear this humiliation he committed suicide by consuming pesticide (reconstructed from Centre for Environment and Food Security 2002).

In Karnataka, a report by Shivaramaiah (2007) for the Karnataka Rajya Raitha Sangha highlights the conditions of degradation among the families in the districts of Mandya, Gulbarga and Bidar where distress-related suicides had taken place. The ten families which were studied closely were all small cultivators who had recently taken to sugarcane cultivation and had borrowed substantial sums for cultivation from non-formal sources. As the support prices for sugarcane declined to Rs 691 per tonne (while the average cost of cultivation per tonne was Rs 1000), the sugarcane factories shuttered down, leaving agriculturists with produce on their fields. The irony of failed labour, capital, and expectations associated with growing sugarcane, is summed up in the report by a comment: "the cane turns into sugar but the sugar fails to turn into money" (Shivaramaiah 2007: 30).

Web of New Risks

Risks of the Market

What we see enveloping agriculturists in their production processes, practices, and impacting their personal and social lives are a web of five types of risks.[8] For the majority of agriculturists, especially marginal and small cultivators, who are already in precarious economic conditions, these risks compound their vulnerability and inability to handle contingencies. Emanating from the neo-liberal agenda and orientation, the spread of 'marketism' to the rural areas is represented by the presence of an unregulated market. Unlike the first phase of the Green Revolution, where the State's procurement policy provided a safety net for production, liberalisation of the economy has enforced multiple risks that are exacerbated with the withdrawal of the State from market regulation. Few cases highlight the impact of this lack of regulation of the commercial agri-business sector than the seeds' markets. Even as production capacity and output of the state seed companies declined, policies encouraged the growth of private, both national and multinational, seed industries to enhance their production capacity and to gain entry into the vast agricultural sector. Focusing on commercial crops such as cotton, tobacco, vegetables, and pulses and cereals, private seed companies have proliferated with little or no regulation of quality and sustainability (Revathi and Murthy 2005). While spurious seeds accounted for production losses in the cultivation of *tur* (red gram), several varieties of vegetables and even cereals, it was particularly so in the context of cultivation of cotton, including that of varieties of Bt cotton. Reports for both Andhra and Maharashtra (Prasad 2003, Citizens' Report 1998) highlight this. The situation is further complicated by the selling of mislabeled, counterfeit seed packets, which often contain more than one variety. One agricultural official was quoted as defining four distinct categories of Bt cotton: "legal, illegal, fake legal and fake illegal." (Sheridan 2009: 9–10). An unregulated seed market seeks to cash in on the demand for new varieties and types of seeds for commercial crops. But as the large number of complaints (Revathi and Murthy 2005) highlight, the quality of most of the seeds is unreliable and in supplying to a largely non-literate and submissive clientele, the seed companies have only enhanced the risks and vulnerabilities of marginal agriculturists.

Yet, such risks are not always recognised in the context in which new hybrid and Bt seeds are introduced and promoted. Kumbamu (2009) describes how farmers in the village of Kadavendi in Warangal district, Andhra Pradesh, took to the cultivation of Bt cotton primarily to increase the productivity of cotton. Gaining near cult status, about 98 per cent of the agriculturists in the village took to Bt cotton cultivation within a period of four years. With large agriculturists taking the lead, many relied completely on the inputs and advice of Bt seed merchants. As Kumbamu (2009) describes, suggested measures such as the use of non-Bt seeds to act as 'refuge plants', to ward off insect attacks etc., are not fully comprehended by agriculturists. The partial implementation of practices often results in exacerbating production risks.

As many agriculturists, including marginal and small cultivators, seek to take to commercial and 'modern' agriculture they are forced to access the market for a range of inputs and services. But the price, availability, quality, and access to a range of inputs, like fertilisers, pesticides, seeds, and machineries are not fully subject to regulation. Important regulatory mechanisms such as process and quality certification, guarantees for seeds and other inputs, safeguard techniques etc., are largely bypassed (Sriram 2006) even as commercial seeds and other inputs such as pesticides and fertilisers gain currency in agricultural production practices. The resulting risks associated with such intrusion and dependency on market-based inputs is elaborated by Sriram (2008) who points out:

> When farming households move from retained seeds to bought-out seeds, one element of control is lost. In moving away from traditional seeds to their hybrid varieties, the crop becomes resource intensive. Though the genetically modified seeds take technology to a higher platform, they require even greater skills. So the farmer loses both ways. If there is an early success, it gets repeated but may be followed by two or more negative fallouts. If the conditions are not as conducive as the first event, then the downside loss is greater than *ex-ante*. Meanwhile with the huge difference in prices between ordinary and research-intensive seeds, the risk of spurious seeds filling the middle price range increases. At the end of this cycle the farmer is unable to figure out why he lost. (Sriram 2008 :176).

Compounding the risks associated with the usage of commercial inputs is the onset of interlinked markets, where private agents and agencies dominate both input (fertilisers, pesticides, machinery, seeds) and output (sale of crops) transactions and also act as creditors. The resulting interlinkages also form a closed circuit in which the sources for credit, production, and marketing, sometimes including credit for non-production expenditure (marriages, health contingencies etc.) are the same, thereby locking agriculturists into relationships of dependency with the creditors. The implications of this are highlighted by Aggarwal (2006) who details the ways in which resource-poor agriculturists in Andhra Pradesh's Telengana belt became victims of this marketism. Even as cultivators took to cotton cultivation they lacked the required technical knowledge, working capital and marketing networks. In such a context, as State support declined, the "...network of private traders rapidly expanded to meet not only the marketing needs of the new crops but also to provide working capital and technical expertise." As a result the "largely unregulated operation of private traders in multiple markets also provided them the opportunity to extract greater surplus from the farmers. Thus, while increased participation in external markets exposed farmers to greater price risks and fraudulent dealings by the private traders, the shrinking role of the State reduced the farmers' ability to cope with these risks"(Aggarwal 2006:1-2).

As agriculturists in the Bijapur (Karnataka) village, where I did field work in 1989 and which I re-studied in 2009,[9] described to me, it is the '*bazaar mandi*' (market people) who they fear and dread the most. Traders, they rue, harass them through the practices of hoarding inputs such as fertilisers and seeds (when supply is scarce), tampering with prices, and adulterating pesticides and fertilisers or selling spurious goods and then failing to pay fair prices when agriculturists seek to sell their produce. P. Sainath's description of Vidarbha and the failure of the 'White Gold' or cotton cultivation in the region captures the conditions that led to acute distress. Compelled by good prices in the 1970s, many agriculturists began cultivating cotton in the dry belts of the Vidarbha. But by the late 1990s, with imported cotton from the USA out-competing local cotton, prices went on a downward spiral.

> By 2005...the living standards of farmers in cotton-growing regions like Vidarbha had fallen sharply. Cotton prices and incomes were crashing,

> debt and cultivation costs soaring. ...On the one hand, cotton growers were locked into the volatility of global prices. On the other, inputs costs were exploding. Local seed cost around Rs 9 per kilogram in 1991. By 2004, commercial seed had taken over and could cost as much as Rs. 1,650 to Rs 1,800 for just 450 grams, thanks to Monsanto's Bt cotton. ...Other inputs, fertilisers, pesticide, utilities like water and electricity, all saw a big rise in costs from the mid to late 1990s. By 2005, cotton prices collapsed. ...By September 2006, farmers in that region were killing themselves. (Sainath 2009: 8).

That such a model of agriculture generates contradictory economic or production conditions is elaborated by Vakulabharanam (2005). In his study of agrarian distress in Andhra Pradesh's Telengana region he indicates how increased input cost of production, which outweighs the output prices, leaves agriculturists in debt[10] and thereby results in 'distress-inducing growth'. That this was relevant for many of the belts which recorded suicides is also made evident in the various testimonials from these regions. Agriculturists in the dry belts of Vidarbha and Telengana tried their hand at various mix and matches of varieties of seeds in cotton and soya; agriculturists in Karnataka switched vegetables from year to year; and those in Punjab alternated between varieties of wheat and/or wheat and rice combinations. Each of these were undertaken in the hope that they would reap profits or at least enable them to break even. Yet, that the market and its vagaries outwitted them have become their common narratives. What emerges from these reports and their details are the new risk-loaded market treadmills which agriculturists ride, believing that each year and each season will break the cycle of loss.

Ecological Risks: Compounding Agriculture as a Gamble

A range of serious ecological risks resulting from the depletion of natural resources is also associated with the promotion of the Green Revolution model. The promotion of water intensive crops in predominantly dry regions, growing ecologically and climatically unsuitable crops, off-season cultivation of crops etc., indicate the extent to which agriculture is increasingly divorced from ecology. Such practices have, then, led to the commodification and privatisation of natural resources, as seen in the proliferation of independently owned tube-wells and the widespread degradation of public resources such as common lands, lakes, tanks and wells.[11] Once well-established, and ecologically fine-tuned, agricultural practices such as mixed crop cultivation of sturdy pulses and cereals have eroded. These shifts in the ownership and use of natural resources and in cultivation patterns and in the forms of relating to the land and to crops (Vasavi 1999) have led to the re-symbolisation of nature/ecology. Far from agricultural resources being collectively owned, appropriated and cared for, capital and specialised/high technology and its know-how have initiated an enhanced separation of natural resources from society.

Although not directly emanating from neo-liberal economic policies but associated with its promotion since the 1990s, are changing climatic conditions. Until recently the agricultural cycle was typically linked to the local ecological pattern which agriculturists knew and understood in depth. However, India's climate, as in other parts of the world and linked largely to global climate change patterns, has witnessed fluctuations in rainfall, changes in its pattern and the alteration in volume and periodicity (Gadgil 2003). These climatic changes have created several problems for agriculturists as there has been a disruption in the established bodies of knowledge, in which there was a close fit between the ecological-agricultural and cultural cycles and practices. Agriculturists are unable to draw on earlier forms of knowledge in cultivating the land or in choosing the appropriate combinations of land quality, climate and crops. Chaotic climate patterns have left many in a state of confusion leading to problems in the management of their lands and crops and in consequent loss of crops or decline in productivity.

Such displacement of local, coping and risk-aversive measures are primarily linked to the fact that "uncertain changes in environmental patterns may remove some of the buffering offered by established coping strategies and institutions based on peasant science and the local tradition of agronomic knowledge and experimentation" (Kasperon and Kasperon 2001: 28). Summaries from several reports and enquiry commissions testify to the extent to which ecological changes, either unexpected heavy rains, or changes in weather conditions, affected production conditions and subsequently led to the inability of agriculturists to handle these conditions or to salvage their standing crops.

"The unusual weather conditions that prevailed in 1997-98 have inflicted severe losses for all the crops due to outbreak of pests, absence of seasonal effects and excessive later rains. In spite of their best efforts to control the pests, farmers were not able to minimise the losses. Though the magnitude of productivity losses (vary) between crops, the effect on cotton proved to be disastrous" (Citizen's Report 1998: 212).

Production Risks

If ecological risks, related to unreliable rainfall, have been recognised as a major source of production risk in Indian agriculture and associated with the stereotyped 'risk aversive' behaviour of Indian agriculturists, then the new agricultural practices have also introduced new production risks. Green Revolution agriculture requires intensive and regular supply of water, which is increasingly becoming a scarce resource. The depletion of the water table itself forms the new risk that most agriculturists face and compounds the risks of indebtedness and loss of crops. In many cases, much of the indebtedness was linked to agriculturists having to dig additional bore wells, as the older ones had run dry. Reports from most of the areas indicate that many of the suicide victims had resorted to having several wells dug on their land (Citizens Report 1998; Galab et al. 2009; Singh 2006).

The Citizens' Report's (1998) details for Warangal district highlight the acute forms of water scarcity which had resulted from intense water mining for cultivation in the region. Cotton growers in the district had relied on deep tube wells and tanks for irrigation, many of which had subsequently run dry. Investments in additional tube wells had been a key source of expenditure and indebtedness. So widespread had the depletion of the water table become that in one village in the district, "...by 1998 there were 1800 bore wells, half of which were dry, and the water table was at 240 feet." (cited in Galab et al. 2009).

In addition, the spread of new crop diseases and pests, linked to the introduction of new crops and fertilisers and the increasing pesticide resistance of some diseases and pests, have led to new risks. Several of the reports and studies have identified the reasons for crop loss being linked to factors such as pest attacks in Maharashtra, Karnataka and in Andhra (Mohanty 2005, Dandekar et al. 2005, Vasavi 1999, Prasad 2003). In Bidar (Vasavi 1999) and Warangal (Toxics Link 2002) large doses of pesticides were required to handle the outbreak of pests such as *heliothesis*.[12]

Risks Related to Accessing Capital

Commercial agricultural cultivation requires increasing amounts of capital and since the late 1990s there has been a severe credit crunch in the rural sectors.[13] National fiscal policies shifted from the directed 'social and development banking' priorities to a competitive regime in which global finance, market-focus, and profitability gained prominence (Ramachandran and Swaminathan 2005). Subsequently, priority lending to agriculture, allocation of funds to rural banks, especially to the agricultural cooperative societies, declined sharply and the rural credit system was subject to a severe squeeze. Data indicates that the proportion of capital allocated to agriculture in total bank credit fell from 19 per cent in 1990 to under 11 per cent in March 2005 (Shah et al. 2007). Such a sharp decline in availability of funds impacted the poor and the marginal agriculturists the most, leading to a decline in the amounts available to them through formal and recognised institutions. In such a context, marginal and small agriculturists had little or no access to capital and had to perforce resort to loans and mortgages as a way to enter into or sustain their commercial cultivation.[14] Recent data from the NSSO (2005b) confirm this indebtedness among agriculturists, particularly among the small and marginal agriculturists and the Backward Classes.[15]

While credit itself is indispensable, as commercial agricultural production requires a range of inputs which are increasingly expensive, the fact that most of these marginal agriculturists lack the social capital to access networks and links to banks and cooperative societies or are considered credit unworthy compounds the risk they take in accessing credit. As a result, many agriculturists access credit from a range of non-institutional credit sources. The Situation Assessment Survey (NSSO 2005a) indicates that only 57.7 per cent of all agriculturists are able to access institutional loans and a large number, especially the small and marginal cultivators are forced to rely on non-institutional sources and therefore bear the burden of higher interest rate loans (Bhalla 2006).

The reports on agriculturists' suicides from the various states indicate that a significant proportion of the suicide victims were indebted and had taken loans from non-institutional sources such as money-lenders, commission agents, dealers of agri-inputs, and relatives and friends. Iyer and Manick (2000) note that in Punjab 67 per cent of the suicide victims were indebted to agricultural commission agents. For Andhra, all the three main reports note the high level of indebtedness to non-institutional agents, and in Maharashtra, Mohanty (2005) notes that most of the small farmers

(83 per cent of the study sample) were indebted to non-institutional agencies. Only in Karnataka, the Experts' Committee Report (2002) notes that 42 per cent of the loans were from the cooperative banks, while 25 per cent were from commercial and regional rural banks and 21 per cent were from moneylenders. Lending rates from money lenders or non-institutional agents has been a key source of debt burden. Rates in Andhra Pradesh ranged from 24 per cent to 36 per cent (Farmers' Welfare Commission 2005; Citizens' Report 1998), while in Karnataka interest rates ranged from 24 per cent to a high 45 per cent in the districts of Bidar and Mandya (Vasavi 2004).

But the debt burden and its impact or association with suicides needs to be contextualised. As several studies have noted and is now common knowledge about Indian agriculture, it is not unusual for agriculturists to be indebted and for them to bear excessive loads of debts, including intergenerational debts. The question that arises is why these contemporary debt burdens have become the source for such distress, subsequently leading to suicides.

Eric Stokes' work (1978) on colonial land and indebtedness provides this historical and comparative perspective. Colonial agrarian indebtedness, associated even then with the expansion of agriculture into new regions and to the production of commercial crops, was also aligned with the relationships between the landlords (zamindars), the money lenders, and the peasants (typically non-landed tenants). Money lenders not only dictated what crops could be grown but also purchased the crops. In times of crises such as loss of crops from droughts or pests it was not unusual for moneylenders to cancel the debts or for indebted cultivators to migrate out. A key difference lies in the fact that in the colonial period most commercial production was led by dominant or upper caste groups who also had considerable leverage with the moneylenders. Backed by substantial networks and ability to mobilise, heavy indebtedness was also occasionally met with agitations against moneylenders and by assertions for state interventions. Unlike the colonial period, where agricultural moneylenders and landed elite were the key agents of usury, currently a significant proportion of debt is disbursed from friends and relatives and the pressure that results from non-payment manifests in higher stress (elaborated in the next chapter).

Agricultural Knowledge Dissonance

In as much as the modern agricultural agenda in India has led to a 'Taylorisation of agriculture' (Visvanathan 1997) it has meant the increasing erosion of the locale specificity of agricultures and agrarian cultures. State and agri-business directed agendas that support market based inputs into agriculture and which seek to alter the very ecological bases of agriculture have promoted the erosion of local practices and knowledge. Local agricultural patterns and practices typically drew from a shared repository of knowledge much of which were transmitted and reproduced through the social and cultural structures of agricultural transactions and practices. However, the new agricultural regimes, from the Green Revolution model's use of hybrid seeds and external inputs to the current use of genetically modified (GM) seeds,[16] induce increasing dissonance between knowledge and know-how. While large and established agriculturists have access to wider and more updated knowledge that is relevant and reliable for their production, the smaller agriculturists, especially newcomers, are unaware of the agro-ecological rationale of their choices. As a result, their "agricultural knowledge …(is) vulnerable to inconsistency, unrecognisability, and overly rapid rates of change in environmental payoffs" (Stone 2007b: 229).

Madhuvanti in her interviews with agriculturists in the village of Tivsa, in Yatwal district (Vidarbha) describes how "only the big, educated farmers who know how to use agro-chemicals properly and who cannot be swindled with spurious seeds and chemicals can manage to get returns from chemical-oriented farming. For farmers who are illiterate and unaware, chemical farming is very risky" (2007: 55). She goes on to detail how marginal agriculturists who took to Bt cotton cultivation, were not fully trained or skilled in the use of associated fertilisers and pesticides (such as Tracer) and subsequently faced tremendous loss of crops and productivity. Such a dissonance in knowledge and know-how indicates a significant shift from not only locally focused knowledge systems but also from the combining of both local and 'modern' practices in even the Green Revolution model (Gupta 1999). In subscribing to new, high productive inputs, such as Bt seeds, the lack of complete knowledge, and the higher investment and risks compound the vulnerability of these agriculturists.

In the context of increasing commercialisation of agriculture, the plurality and intensity of competition among agri-business players have meant that they resort to multiple ways to promote their products and attract and retain agriculturists as their clients. Apart from promoting hoardings and advertisements that promise manifold bounties and successful production, such agencies conduct on-site 'field parties' which include demonstrations and promotions of seeds, technologies, and inputs in the fields of successful agriculturists. In what was unknown even a decade ago, agriculturists are invited to such 'field parties' which include not only a demonstration or discussion related to new inputs and practices, but also a good meal and to a showcasing of the field owner as a leader and an entrepreneur. In making, marking and promoting the new forms of commercial agriculture and the potential to be successful agriculturists, the agri-business agents and the agencies act as both economic and social promoters engaging in and facilitating new economic and social aspirations and mobilities. Their significance as agents not only of change but as also reinforcing existing structures of power and privilege are often overlooked and only rarely is it recognised that "aggressive marketing strategies such as demonstration plots are not simply neutral experiments in the field but are interwoven with power relations and social relations, which thereby reinforce inequities in the rural society" (Kumbamu: 2009: 35).

The promotion and spread of new practices are increasingly dictated by market-led 'fads' (Stone 2007) in which agriculturists purchase inputs based on what is popular. This and the intense competition among agriculturists to out compete others by using new commercial varieties of seeds, fertilisers, and pesticides accounts for the subscription to practices and inputs which eventually harm the cultivators. Stone's (2007) description of this among cotton cultivators in Andhra Pradesh is apposite; far from the earlier forms of contextualised learning that was environmentally based, recent learning is primarily sourced from agri-business agencies and has led to the increasing 'de-skilling' of agriculturists – an inability to be able to cultivate crops with appropriate and relevant skills.

Although commercial and high external input agricultural models are being promoted, there is little or no systematic dissemination of information, knowledge and training provided to agriculturists. Data from the NSSO Survey No. 499 (2005) indicates the absence of public agencies in rural India and the lack of knowledge dissemination to a significant proportion of people. Only 8.4 per cent of agriculturists had accessed information from the *Krishi Vigyan Kendra*s (farmers Science Centres) and 17 per cent received information from other agriculturists and 13 per cent from agricultural input dealers. Many of the reports and studies (Citizens' Report 1998, Vasavi 1999, Mohanty 2005; Kumbamu 2009), also mention the inability of the cultivators to use appropriate knowledge and skills related to the new commercial inputs particularly pesticides as a reason for their problems in agriculture. Toxics Link's report (2002) on deaths from pesticide exposure describes the range of unsafe ways in which pesticides are applied and pesticide containers are used for domestic and cooking purposes, thereby leading to various pesticide related health hazards and deaths. In addition, the lack of knowledge of appropriate doses of pesticides has been a leading cause for increasing debts as agriculturists purchased and sprayed unnecessarily large amounts of pesticides on their field.

In adopting the new agricultural knowledge and techniques there is an erosion of local knowledge that also leads to the loss of the 'culture of everyday life' (Gorz 1993: 57). That is, knowledge and know-how that refers to "the whole self-evident collection of intuitive knowledge or vernacular know-how … the habits, norms and modes of conduct that enable individuals to interpret, to understand, to assume responsibility for the way they inhabit the work that surrounds them" (Gorz 1993:57) is no longer in function. The result is a loss of both autonomy and identity that further erodes the reproduction of localised and varied agri-cultural formations.

Social Implications of Risk

Increasing indebtedness, lack of marketing support, unviable parcels of land and the inability to provide basic support to cater to the family's requirements mark the lives of those attempting to sustain themselves within this dominant model. Such risks are significant for marginalised and small agriculturists who form the bulk of the agrarian population. The increasing commercialisation of agriculture, the subscription to the dominant Green Revolution model, the range of risks, and the knowledge dissonance indicate the overall negative impact of the Green Revolution for marginal areas and for marginalised agriculturists who attempt to adopt new, commercial agricultural practices. There is, as several studies have indicated,[17] a decline in productivity, growing cost of production, and increasing environmental degradation. As production costs outweigh sale and support prices, and as environmental problems of inadequate water, spread of crop pests and diseases recur and as the market brings no remunerative prices, the condition of the average agriculturist has deteriorated.

In summary, what the new agricultural regime has meant in most tracks of the country and especially to marginal and small cultivators is that of facilitating the free hand of the market, removing regulatory mechanisms and the risk-scaffolding structures (Sanyal 2008; Kumbamu 2009; Shah 2010). In overlooking the multiple risks that most agriculturists face and in the promotion of market-based and market-dependent models there has been scant attention paid to the increasing capability decline of all agriculturists and the vulnerability of marginal cultivators.

Indian agriculture, for long represented as 'a gamble in the monsoons', is now, in the phase of expedited globalisation, an enhanced checkered game, with multiple risks and hurdles. As a result, "...the Indian farmer is at the receiving end. He is in an enterprise where the entrepreneur is not insulated from the enterprise. While in the formal industrial sector, due to the limited liability clause, the entrepreneur is generally insulated from failure, this is not so in agriculture. The inappropriate risk mitigation products also indicate that there are no effective external remedies. The results of such intense forms of risks mean that the costs are often borne by the agriculturists themselves" (Sriram 2008: 178). Symbolically, for many agriculturists, the new agriculture is a beacon of a new future, but in reality it consists of several visible and invisible barriers that facilitate and ensure success to only a few. In as much as the new agriculture encodes these multiple risks, it also encapsulates personal risk as a key category in the lives of agriculturists. From the economic (risks associated with capital and market), ecological (emanating from variable and unpredictable rainfall, declining water levels, spread of plant diseases) to those of social risks (knowledge and networking), every agriculturist, especially those from the marginal caste and class groups, faces the threat of being personally entrapped in this web of risks. The implications of this become significant not merely for production but also for the very relationship of the agriculturalist to her or his land and crops, to the nature of the society in which they live, and for their own lives. Crop loss becomes not merely a source of economic distress but also a deep sense of erosion of one's own self.

Recent sociological scholarship recognises risk as a condition that significantly marks societies, especially Western, democratic ones, from the late twentieth century onwards.[18] Emanating primarily from the gathering problems of ecological changes and environmental degradation in the post-industrial West, the risks that have been identified include that of the spread of markets, the withdrawing State, altering livelihoods, restructuring families, the spread of new knowledges and technologies etc. Yet, as Rustin has pointed out, this recent recognition of risk as "a new societal condition" (1994: 349) overlooks the long existing structural risks of poverty, deprivation, and disadvantage which envelop large numbers of societies. This is relevant for India, where the structural bases of agriculture, its embeddedness in the iniquitous caste system, the dependence on the highly erratic monsoon, the very precarious production conditions of agriculture, and the unreliable delivery of a range of welfare programmes have only compounded the immense and multiple forms of disadvantage that the resource and land poor and low-ranked caste groups face. Hence while one can draw on the observations and implications of what is entailed in a 'risk society', it is important for us to qualify the prevailing theories and highlight the new and additional burdens of risks, the increasing "complexification of risk" (Crook 1999: 181) that agriculturists in general and marginal and small agriculturists in particular have to bear in the context of altering economic regimes.

Several factors including unreliable agricultural inputs, the need to rely on usurious debts to pay for these inputs, and the gaps between the new knowledge required to produce new or commercial crops or crops from new seeds mean that risks are compounded in the engagement with or entry into commercial agriculture. As a result, these webs of risk locate agriculturists in precarious positions and make agriculture a more risk-laden endeavor than ever before. The absence of both, customary support structures and State support programmes, further erode the ability of agriculturists to bear losses over seasons and over the years.

Agriculture under the conditions of neo-liberal political economy entails a higher and deeper investment of the individual. In addition to exercising choices, made primarily on the basis of the promises and potential of the new agriculture models, agriculturists invest their own selves (their pride, relationships, their standing and reputation), their knowledge and know-how, expend their own labour and integrate family labour, liquidate their assets, and extend themselves through seeking alliances and support through new networks. For individuals caught within the limitations of caste and class disadvantage, the promise of a new way of life is embodied in the possibility of new cultivation methods, growing new crops and engaging in the market. All of these hold the potential of new and higher sources of income, and thereby new lifestyles and new identities.

Engaging in commercial cultivation of crops contains within itself dual possibilities; the promise of breaking out of deprivation and the threat of absolute ruin. In experiencing and being caught in the web of risks that include old and new ones, agriculturists are faced with multiple burdens in which the very viability of agriculture and their own livelihoods stand threatened.

In many ways, the Green Revolution in all its phases in India represents a case of the 'gardening posture' (Bauman 2001: 269) of modernity, directed by the government in which the landscape, land, homesteads, and the people have been subject to the imprints of an artificial, rationally designed physical order. As a model for agricultural growth and of even rural development, the promoters of the Green Revolution model and now of an advanced version under the neo-liberal dispensation, have successfully avoided addressing the problems of resource distribution, the caste-embeddedness of India's agrarian structure, (and the promise of inclusive economic growth and social development) and have primarily seen agricultural development as a growth in productivity with 'productivity' (measured in output amounts per hectare and in total volume of production) made a trope for development itself. That the model itself has gone awry is indicated in the extent to which even the limited islands of growth and productivity, the regions identified as the Green Revolution belts such as the Punjab have also become its victims. There is, as several studies have indicated,[19] a decline in productivity, growing cost of production, and increasing environmental degradation of agricultural land all across the nation, especially in the Green Revolution belts, all of which have been attendant with the spread and intensification of environment-based illnesses. Travelling in the Punjab, considered the grain basket of the nation, Newman (2007) identified three interrelated problems in the region: that of increasing inequality between groups; an economic collapse of small cultivation units; and increasing indebtedness among most agriculturists.

As reports and studies of suicides from the various states describe and highlight, it is the marginal agriculturists who are primarily the victims of the new agricultural regime and who are now facing and bearing the multiple burdens associated with high risk agricultural practices. And in the context of the lack of support from the State and in the altering conditions of their own sociality and identities, many of them have been rendered into conditions of deeper depredation and immiseration. Under such conditions, what needs to be explicated and contextualised is why and how suicide has become the dominant way out and trope with which to escape from the multiple burdens of agriculture. For the web of risks imprint agriculturists in multiple ways: ecological risks in as much as the model of agriculture depletes local resources and defies ecological specificity; as economic risks that encapsulate and enmesh agriculturists into external circuits and demands of capital and credit; and as personal risks, that become loaded as social and psychological burdens, and which constitute and entail for the marginal agriculturists the defining terms in which they must conduct agriculture and also their lives.

Notes

1 Official or government appointed committee-based reports are available only for Punjab (IDC 1998), Karnataka (Government of Karnataka 2002) and for Andhra Pradesh (Commission on Farmers' Welfare 2005), and the one for Maharashtra (Dandekar et al. 2005). For Gujarat, the state government has officially denied the prevalence of suicides among agriculturists but this has been contested by reporters and scholars. The other reports or essays are studies by various commissions set up by independent agriculturists groups (e.g. for Andhra Pradesh the ones by the Citizens Report 1998 and the Farmers Commission of Experts 2002) and by independent scholars (e.g. Mishra 2006). A comprehensive overview with a focus on Andhra is also provided by the report commissioned by Christian Aid (Christian Aid 2005) and the work by Galab et al. (2009). Since 2004 a number of essays pertaining to the suicides have been published and these are represented in the journal, the *Economic and Political Weekly*, and a composite book on the theme is that by Reddy and Mishra (2009).

2 A broad structure of agricultural production, which draws primarily on the caste system and is relevant for most regions of India has been delineated in the previous chapter. Here I draw on Shahid Amin's seminal essay (1982) which argues for recognizing the 'production process', and hence the linkages between agriculturists and the ecological specificities, actual tasks, deployment of labour, and immediate demands and pressures of production in different contexts.

3 Policy focus and shifts in relation to agriculture as discernable over the different periods. From 1947-57 the focus was on institutional reforms, land reforms and the establishment of irrigation and agricultural infrastructure. Over the 1960s, the emphasis shifted to the establishment

of agricultural universities, laboratories and the extension service. Over the 1970s attention focused on promoting the Green Revolution model into various regions and in the 1980s the new technology missions and targeted programmes gained mainstay. The post 1991 period saw a clear shift away from land reforms and towards decentralised development. In the years, 2002-2007, there was visible decline in public investment in infrastructure and irrigation, decline in the agricultural extension services, and decline in the availability of credit. (Compiled from various sources; Vaidyanathan 2006, Reddy and Mishra 2009; Bhalla and Singh 2009).

4 There are now several studies that detail the impact of the post 1991 agricultural policies on agriculture and agriculturists. Some of the key ones are those by Vaidyanathan (2006); Bhalla (2006); Balakrishnan et al. (2008), and Reddy and Mishra (2009), and Bhalla and Singh (2009).

5 Since agriculture is on the state list, each regional state is responsible for formulating and working out specific policies but the outlines and non-negotiable parameters are often set by the centre which controls fiscal policies and also formulates the dominant policies.

6 The second phase of the Green Revolution (1980-83 to 1990-93) refers to the phase in which there has been the promotion of the Green Revolution into the semi-arid areas and the focus on cultivation of hybrid seeds in non-cereal crops such as sorghum, pulses, vegetables and fruits. The term the 'Second Green Revolution' or GR II is used to refer to the focus and promotion of new seeds varieties such as genetically modified (GM) seeds that are used in the cultivation of crops such as cotton and more recently that of brinjals in India.

7 The Agricultural Census Division, Ministry of Agriculture, Government of India classifies landholding as follows: Marginal (less than 1 hectare), Small (1 to 2 hectares), Semi-Medium (2 to 4 hectares), Medium (4 to 10 hectares), Large (more than 10 hectares). All data sourced from http://agricoop.nic.in/statistics.

For the states which reported high suicides among agriculturists, the everage landholding size (in hectares) was reported: Punjab: 3.79; Maharashtra: 1.87; Kerala: 0.27; Karnataka: 1.95; Andhra Pradesh: 1.36. The all-India average size of holding was 1.41 hectares (2001 census) and has declined to 1.33 hectares (NSSO 2005).

8 Surjit Singh (2008) identifies five types of risks faced by agriculturists

in the context of a liberalised economy. These five risks are that of production or yield risk, price and market risks, institutional or policy risks, human risks, and financial risks.

9 I first conducted fieldwork in Madhbavi village in Bijapur district, a semi-arid region, of Karnataka in 1989-90 for my dissertation work. Although I visited the village periodically, I conducted a formal study again in January 2009 to take stock of the changes that were taking place in the region and its society.

10 For more details see the excellent essay by Vamsi Vakulabharanam (2005) as it provides an overarching economic and social perspective on the contradictory production conditions which have become prevalent in vast regions of the country.

11 Several revisit studies (see footnote number 16 Chapter II) note the degradation of public resources in various regions. For details of such degradation see periodic reports in the magazine *Down to Earth.*

12 *Heliothesis,* a plant eating pest, most commonly found in pulses such as red gram. Also called *helicoverpa.*

13 The lack of availability of credit has been stressed by studies such as that by Ramachandran and Swaminathan (2005), Bhalla (2006). A summative and critical study is that by Mihir Shah et al. (2007).

14 A proportion of the loans undertaken by the victims (varying across the states) were for non-agricultural and non-productive purposes. Investment in education and expenses on health and social obligations also constitute a key source of debt burden. As the Report of the Commission on Farmers' Welfare elaborates, "…health seeking behaviour as well as the educational aspirations of farmers have changed, and the public systems cannot cater to this new situation, there are skyrocketing health and education expenditures driving the farmers into deeper debt traps" (2005:111).

15 The NSSO 55th Round (1999-2000) indicates complex trends; for one incidence of indebtedness among all rural labour households had declined from 35 per cent in 1993-94 to 25 per cent in 1999-2000 but the average debt per indebted household had increased by 90 per cent. Castes identified as 'OBC' (Other Backward Classes) had a higher incidence of indebtedness than other households and new sources of credit such as shopkeepers, friends and relatives and cooperative societies had emerged

as significant players. Marginal agriculturists had higher share of loans.

16 The introduction and use of GM seeds in India is primarily related to Bt cotton and attempts are now being made to introduce Bt brinjal and Bt corn.

17 There are now several studies that highlight the negative fall-outs of the Green Revolution in India. Key studies include those by Omvedt (1992) and Shiva (1991).

18 Schools of thought that have addressed and focused on 'risk' as a key aspect of society can be identified as falling into three camps: that by Douglas and Widavsky on the cultural construction of risk; the body of debates and discussions initiated by Giddens and then by Ulrich Beck; and studies drawing on Foucault (see Lipton 1999). I have drawn primarily on sociological and social anthropological studies with a focus on the social burdens of new risks especially in the context of increasing individualisation. Works by Norbert Elias (1991) and Ulrich Beck (1999) have been seminal to the arguments explicated here.

19 See studies by Sukhpal Singh (2000), Ramesh Chand (1999) and others for Punjab.

Those who have much land and money are not with the headaches of agriculture. Those who live by their labour are getting by with new jobs and more money. But, it is us, the middle agriculturists… we bear the load of cultivating with poor seeds, waiting for the rains, being at the mercy of the trader and the creditors.

Ravi Biradar, Madhbhavi Village, 2009

Social crises appear as individual crises, which are no longer (or are very indirectly) perceived in terms of their rootedness in the social realm.

Ulrich Beck, *World Risk Society*, 1999

Chapter Four

Agricultural Individualisation and Social Entrapment

> ...the farmers under distress are heavily indebted due to various government policies. The creditors subjected these farmers to various indignities and humiliation. Some of the farmers under unbearable distress conditions, with the fear of losing their only source of livelihood, i.e, the land they were tilling, and in the process of discharging their debts, committed suicide for which the government policies are responsible
>
> **Report of the Farmers' Commission of Experts on Agriculture in Andhra Pradesh, 2002**

Reports from the states most affected by the suicides indicate that most of the victims were marginal[1] (less than 1 hectare) and small (1 to 2 hectares) cultivators, followed by semi-medium (more than 2, upto 4 hectares) cultivators. With the exception of the Punjab where a sizeable number (45 per cent according to IDC [1998] and 31 per cent by Iyer and Manick [2000]) of the victims were landless, the numbers from the extremes of the range, i.e the landless and the large holders in the other states were minimal. Details from the reports indicate that in Andhra Pradesh, among those who committed suicide in Warangal, Guntur, and Anantapur districts between the years of 1997-98, most (86 per cent) owned or operated less than four acres of land and about 40 per cent of all the victims had leased-in land (Citizens' Report 1998; Prasad 2003). In Karnataka, most of the victims from the districts of Bidar, Hassan and Mandya were small agriculturists with an average of two hectares (Vasavi

1999; 2004). The Expert Committee, appointed by the Government of Karnataka, also indicates that most (44 per cent) of the victims were small landholders, where 32 per cent had leased in land and the average land holding of the victims was 5.44 acres (Government of Karnataka 2002). Similarly, for Maharashtra, Mohanty's (2005) study of Amravati and Yavatmal districts indicates that most (64 per cent) of the victims were small cultivators with less than four hectares of land and who supplemented agricultural income with wage labour. The TISS report (Dandekar et al. 2005) indicates that a majority (80 per cent) were small (upto 5 acres) and medium (between 5 to 15 acres) cultivators, while only 13 per cent were large (more than 15 acres) cultivators. Similarly, Mishra's (2006) study of Maharashtra records 53 per cent of the victims as having less than five acres, 20 per cent with landholdings between 2-10 acres and only 3 per cent as having more than 20 acres. For Wayanad district in Kerala, Mohanakumar and Sharma (2006) report that 47 per cent of the agriculturists had less than one acre of land and the rest were cultivators with landholdings between 2 to 6 acres each. For Punjab, the IDC report (1998) on the districts of Gurdaspur, Sangrur, Mansa and Ludhiana indicates that 24 per cent of the victims were marginal and small cultivators, while 24 per cent were semi-medium cultivators, and only 5 per cent were large cultivators. The report by Iyer and Manick (2000) for Sangrur district indicates that 54 per cent of the victims were from small cultivating families (less than five acres).

Caste background of the Victims

Compounding such economic marginality is the fact that a significant proportion of the suicide victims were from 'Backward Classes'[2] or from lower ranked caste groups. In Andhra Pradesh, two-thirds of the victims in Warangal were from the 'Backward Class' groups of Yadava, Chakali, Telaga, Wadla, Mangali, Padmashali and Lambada (Citizens' Report 1998; Venkateshwarlu 1998). In Anantapur district most of the victims were from the non-agricultural castes of Sale, Besta and Uppara although there were some from the traditional cultivating castes such as the Reddy and Baliga. In Maharashtra's Amravati and Yavatmal districts, most were also from the middle or non-cultivating castes of Telis, Beldars and Banjara or from the Scheduled communities of Mahar, Nav-Buddha, Matang, Chamar, and Dhangar (Mohanty 2005). For Vidarbha and Marathwada regions, the TISS report (Dandekar et al. 2005) identified a spread across the caste groups but a predominant number were from the 'Other Backward Classes'[3] (27 per cent) and the other non-scheduled caste groups (36 per cent). With details for 390 households which had suicides related to agricultural distress, Mishra documents that a significant proportion (44 per cent) belonged to the OBC groups with the Kunbis among them accounting for the largest per cent while among the *vimukta jati* and nomadic tribes it was the Banjara who accounted for 16 per cent of suicides. Other castes, such as Marathas and Rajputs recorded only 6 per cent of suicides. Matching the proportion of suicide victims to that of the general population in each of the regions indicates varied trends. While the caste composition in the Vidarbha and the Telangana region consists of a predominance of 'Backward Class' groups, the districts of Wayanad and Idukki of Kerala have a mixed population including the state's highest proportion of tribals/Adivasis.

For Punjab, the southern districts, most affected by suicides also record a mixed population with high proportion of Jat Sikhs. For Karnataka, where the suicides were spread across the state, the caste background of the victims coincides with the landholding pattern of the varied caste groups. Hence, as differing from Maharashtra and Andhra Pradesh, the caste background of victims from Punjab and Karnataka indicates variations. For Punjab, the IDC report (1998) records that a significant proportion (71 per cent) were Sikhs while the report by Iyer and Manick (2000) notes that 63 per cent of the victims were Jat Sikhs, 10 per cent were Jat Hindus, 9 per cent were Backward Classes and 17.5 per cent were Scheduled Castes. In Karnataka, in the districts of Mandya and Hassan most of the victims were from the dominant Vokkaliga community (Vasavi 2004) and only a small proportion were from the Backward Classes.[4] But, the land holding pattern indicates that most were small and medium agriculturists with limited land holding.

Some of the regions, such as Vidarbha in Maharashtra, Warangal and Guntur districts in Andhra Pradesh, and Patiala in the Punjab, were also witnessing small openings in the agrarian social structure. Over the years, the integration of the dominant castes into urban, professional and/or business enterprises and their withdrawal and absence from agricultural operations had created opportunities for middle-rank and non-cultivating caste groups to take to cultivation. In addition, some new government programmes which facilitated access to land had created opportunities for middle ranking and lower castes to gain entry into 'modern' and capital-based agriculture. Such shifts also account for the fact that a significant proportion of the distressed families in these regions were also from these new but marginal cultivating households.

The Burdens of Marginality

Contrary to popular constructions, most of the victims have not been the most poor or destitute, or those who are still retained in conditions of subsistence agriculture and/or in the poorest regions of the nation (as in Bihar, the heartland of Uttar Pradesh etc.). Instead, the overwhelming numbers of the victims have been small cultivators in the belts where commercial agriculture has spread and intensified. The conditions and experiences of most of the victims as documented and detailed in the reports and studies of the suicides represent the life of the majority of cultivators who are also marginalised in multiple ways. Trends of decreasing land size and decreasing availability of work have meant that large numbers of agriculturists have become subject to processes of pauperisation and resource depletion, and are also bearers of increasing burdens. Their position in the local and macro economy is one of marginality, not merely from their ownership or cultivation of limited plots and sizes of land but also from the marginal political and social position they occupy in the immediate and larger political economies of the nation. What Sanyal (2008) and Akram-Lodhi and Kay (2009) identify as markers of marginality is valid for all these households. In addition to limited land holding, marginal cultivators suffer from insecurity of ownership and tenancy, produce for both consumption and the market, are structurally situated in conditions where the surplus production is often transferred to dominant classes, and are subject to processes of semi-proletarianisation and proletarianisation. Additionally, most marginal cultivators are also from the lower-ranked jatis and subsequently lack the social and cultural capital to emerge as successful or entrepreneurial agriculturists. Over the years, vast amounts of research have highlighted how the 'fall-back position' of marginal agricultural households is influenced by factors such as the ownership and control over assets, access to employment, income generation, common property resources, and availability of external structures of support from kinship and informal circles and from that of the State (Agarwal 1997). Despite this, dominant policies and programmes continue to ignore their needs and requirements, enforcing upon marginal cultivators enhanced forms of marginality which include multiple forms of exclusion, exploitation, oppression, and discrimination (John 2010). Marginality then results in the persistent non-recognition of the needs of these resource-poor cultivators and an 'invisibilisation' of their presence in the economic planning imaginary. Given their marginality, it is important to discern how the 'web of risks' impacted them and made them more vulnerable than even the 'subsistence' cultivators or the landless workers.

While several studies have indicated the increasing pauperisation and de-peasantisation processes that impact small and marginal cultivators,[5] the cases of suicides underscore the ways in which economically and socially marginal families are attempting to either stall or overcome their conditions of impoverishment and/or disadvantage and are attempting to enhance their incomes and standards of living. In their attempts to sustain or enhance their livelihoods many of the marginal agriculturists attempt to shift from predominantly non-commercial cultivation and gain entry into commercial production with a focus on marketing their produce.

For some others, such as the artisan and service *jati*s the declining availability and sustainability of agriculture and village related occupations compel them to move into agriculture from non-agricultural occupations and livelihoods. What the cases indicate is the attempt by members of small and marginal holdings (either owned or rented), who may combine small holdings with labour on others' lands, to gain a foothold into commercial agriculture and thereby improve their livelihoods and standard of living. Such strategies have been necessitated by the loss of their traditional occupations through the introduction of machines and new technologies, the integration of agriculture into the market economy and the displacement of rural products by industrial products. Members of artisan, service and craft groups such as potters, wheel-makers, smiths, basket makers and others have particularly been impacted by such trends. Until recently such groups have had to perforce resort to becoming agricultural labourers or migrating to seek livelihoods and employment in a diversity of occupations in varied settings.

Case studies[6] from across the states provide evidence to the marginality of these agriculturists and the degraded conditions in which they practice agriculture. From Andhra Pradesh, the Citizens' Report (1998) describes the condition of one such agriculturist:

> Kanugula Sambaiah, 38 years old, of Shambaiahpally, belonged to the Potter Caste and was educated upto Std VIII. He had a holding of three acres, which were rain dependent, and he cultivated chillies in 10 *guntas* and cotton in the rest. He had accumulated a debt of Rs. 80,000 until the summer of 1997. He purchased pesticide from a dealer in a nearby village. He found it to be spurious and unable to control the pests. Having lost all his crops, he and his wife were reduced to working as casual labourers. According to his wife, Sambaiah used to cry while looking at the crops. Finally, he chose to die and his wife remains without a way out of the debts that have mounted.

In Maharashtra, the conditions of one of the families in a village where agriculturists had resorted to suicide are described by Madhumati (2007:14) as follows:

> Janardhan Krishaji Gondhare, a Dalit agriculturist, owns seven acres of unirrigated land in Dorli in Wardha District. He shifted from 'traditional' agriculture and currently cultivates cotton on four acres and the remaining is used for cultivating soya. He was induced to take to the new agriculture, especially to growing Bt cotton, by the advertisements of seed companies. He had borrowed ten thousand rupees from the local moneylender who also sells agricultural inputs, and who had to be repaid in six months with fifteen thousand rupees. But the cotton yield was low, primarily due to pest attacks. Gondhare incurred further losses when the cotton was sold at low market prices and he was under pressure to repay the money lender. As a result, Gondhare made no profit and has incurred losses over several years. Despondent, he confesses to wanting to leave agriculture.

Many agricuturists, having expended much effort and capital on commercial agriculture, face forms of humiliation. From Punjab, where suicides had peaked between 1998 and 2000, Manick and Iyer (2000) describe one such case:

> Pala Singh, a Jat Sikh aged 28 years, with two acres of own land had leased in another two acres on a sharecropping basis. His own land did not have a bore well and he had borrowed from a commission agent (rupees sixty thousand at twenty-four per cent interest rate) and Rs. fifteen thousand from close relatives. He had not been able to repay the loans, and the commission agent had begun to harass him.

> He consumed poison and died. He leaves behind his aged mother, a wife and a young child.

The official report for the Government of Maharashtra (Dandekar et al. 2005) on the suicides in the Vidarbha region elaborates on another case where a marginal agriculturist had resorted to suicide:

> Vinod Rathore committed suicide in 2000 after drinking pesticide. He had taken loans from Banks and the recovery officials had humiliated him in public. The Bank officials had also threatened to confiscate the household goods and Vinod had poisoned himself after this threat. The oldest daughter has dropped out of tenth standard and his wife, Baby, is now concerned about getting her married. Compensation from the State is awaited.

The report also records the conditions of a Scheduled Caste woman agriculturist who had resorted to suicide:

> The household head was looking after all the agrarian operations and managing a landholding of 15 acres. The family purchased six acres of the land in the year 1969 through savings from earnings doing labour. The major crops were cotton, tur and jowar. The eldest son in the family is a vegetable vendor and the younger son has slight mental disability. The husband of the household head has been physically disabled for the last 15 years. The entire burden of decision-making in the context of agrarian operations had fallen on the female household head alone.

The case of an agriculturist from a denotified tribe who, in his attempt to expand his cultivation and engage with commercial agriculture, faced loss and an inability to repay agriculture-related debt is described in the report by IGIDR (Mishra 2006).

> Belonging to the denotified tribe community, the family has total holdings of three acres of dry land and the family had been leasing in seven acres since the past five years. Initially the family's economic condition improved but the last (2004) crop failed and the man defaulted on his loans. He owed money to a bank, a cooperative society, and private moneylenders. He had also invested his savings on cultivation and had to sell his motorbike and a pair of bullocks to

manage his agricultural commitments. He committed suicide and compensation has not been disbursed.

Comparison between Households

Details of the specific conditions of the households of victims and their differences from others in the villages are elaborated by two studies for the Vidarbha region of Maharashtra, and one for the Punjab. For Maharashtra, Mohanty and Shroff's study (2004) indicates that the victims' households had higher proportions of loans from non-institutional sources, fewer assets to dispose of when they were unable to pay off loans, higher educational qualifications than others in the village, were single or individual decision-makers and managers of their land, and had more social problems such as alcoholism,[7] tensions in the family etc., than the other households that were compared. Srijit Mishra's study (2006) indicates the differences between the victims' families and those families that had similar economic positions in the villages of Maharashtra. Most of the victims were from nuclear families but with larger than average number of family members, (especially more women of marriageable age, and therefore the family head bore the burden of arranging dowries), with higher proportions of debts, lower access to basic amenities, and lesser ownership of assets than the other households. Grover et al. (2008) provide a similar comparative picture for the Punjab. Most of the victims families had lower assets, higher debts with a higher proportion from non-institutional sources, and a higher incidence of family troubles as compared with the control group.

If undertaking or switching to commercial agriculture resulted in the intensification of risks and vulnerabilities, and therefore led to an erosion of the capabilities of these marginal households, then the question of the significance of such commercial agriculture and its impact on the life conditions of marginal agriculturists needs to be raised. A result of the introduction of new and market-driven forms of knowledge, and its attendant restructuring of agrarian social relations and the emergence of new class formations, is the significant alteration in the life-world of agrarian communities. Agriculturists in general and marginal agriculturists in particular are typically associated with resilience and work capacities that indicate their abilities to maximise even basic or rudimentary resources. They represent in many ways the 'self-exploitation' of agriculturists that account for both their resilience and their ability to reproduce the domestic unit as a unit of production and reproduction.[8] Such work and engagement often hid the many forms and degrees of self-exploitation that most agriculturists submit to. But, the erosion of this ability to survive or reproduce the cultivating unit represents the new social constitution of the practice of agriculture and thereby the social positioning of the individual, especially the marginal agriculturist.

Agricultural Individualisation

The increasing integration of agriculturists into the market economy has led to reordering the cultural basis of Indian agriculture.[9] Although it is well-known and established that the agrarian system has long been hierarchical with caste-based allocation of rights over land and its resources, regional agricultural practices were conducted on a pattern of collectively shared knowledge forms and on shared rhythms. As other studies have elaborated, agriculture in the non-commercial context was conducted on shared knowledge systems which included negotiating old and new agricultural know-how, drawing on networks of kin and fellow workers, and related to in terms that had cultural significance (Boehm 2003). Typically, agriculture was a combination of 'social performance' (Richards 1993) conducted by drawing on social relations and networks and also a 'planned set of strategies' (Batterbury 1996) with which agriculturists made decisions, choices, and engaged in activities.[10] In addition, the patterns and production processes by which agriculture was undertaken was on region-specific patterns in which all agriculturists, irrespective of class and caste differences (and differences in size of holdings), conducted agriculture to suit local ecological conditions. Regional or agro-ecology specific agriculture was based on a society-nature relationship in which society relied on a corpus of collective knowledge to appropriate nature within a range of hierarchical social and economic structures and relationships.[11] While the structure of social activities was itself linked to the ecological and agricultural cycles, the key idioms and terms of cultural life were drawn from and linked to agricultural activities. Even as agriculture was based on differential rights and status, it provided a larger collective identity to a range of people who performed different functions in its working.

But a combination of factors has introduced significant shifts in the patterns and practices of agriculture. For one, the commercialisation of agriculture has introduced the use of external inputs and practices that are not locally derived or evolved. Those with larger holdings of land and with access to market and capital are now able to practice forms of agriculture which are derived from norms and expectations stipulated to them by agricultural extension agents or increasingly by agri-business and credit agents. Each agriculturist now competes with the other to enhance productivity or grow the new crops that fetch the best market prices. This has not only meant the distancing of local practices of agriculture which draw from commonly known and transmitted forms of cultivation but also to the distancing of agriculturists from each other. As Stone (2007a) notes, the swamping of agricultural markets with new commercial agencies and outlets and their keen competition for new buyers and players has led to intense competition among agriculturists. This in turn has led to an erosion of both, the mixing and matching of the social and symbolic (which were typical characteristics of agriculture in its earlier phase) and new forms of planning (see Vasavi 1999, Gupta 1999). As individual players, agriculturists must seek knowledge, credit, and access the market on an individual basis thereby individually bearing a larger burden of the web of risks than they would have in the context of agriculture as embedded in the local ecological-cultural world. Plans and strategies which are afforded by or are available to dominant castes, primarily land-owning, or cultivating castes are not within access to the low-ranked or new agricultural players.

That agriculture in India drew on a network of relationships in which cooperation and extension of assistance for a range of activities formed part of the production processes itself has been noted by key scholars (Amin 1982; Breman 2007). With changes induced by commercialisation of agriculture the caste-based social bases of production[12] have been largely retained while the support and sustenance that could have been provided during times of crisis under the patron-client systems have disintegrated (Breman 2007; Vasavi 1999). As a result, collective strategies of risk management and alleviation of distress that were forms of adaptations to droughts and periodic scarcity of resources and production loss are largely eroded and in many cases "...all adaptations/adjustment mechanisms that derived their strength from social relations and the community's collective approach are less feasible" (Jodha 2001: 55) now. Such trends have further eroded the household and individual capacities of marginal agriculturists to make a living or sustain their families. Sociologically, such erosion of local practices of agriculture and the corpus of rituals associated with them have significance for the constitution and working of the societies themselves. As interdependence based on customary structures declines, dependence on external structures and agencies increases. But growing dependence is not always met with assurances of provisioning and support. While the disintegration of customary forms of support has also liberated the working, low-ranked caste groups and enabled them to escape from caste prescribed subservience and debt servicing, the provisioning mechanisms of the moral economy have not been adequately replaced by State mechanisms of provisioning. Factionalism and lack of accountability of the bureaucracies that administer State provisioning have meant that allocations to the most deserving rarely reach them (Chatterjee 2009 ; Shah 2010). What Jodhka identifies as "autonomisation from the 'traditional' rural economy and structures of patronage and loyalty" (2005: 22) has combined with the continued prejudice of the upper castes against the former untouchable caste groups and has increased the social isolation of the low ranking agriculturists. If taking to commercial and market-dependent agriculture led to knowledge dissonance, then for those taking to agriculture as a new occupation the situation is doubly hazardous. Many cases of the suicide victims were representative of such shifts in occupation. Mohanty (2005) highlights the tensions that arise from low-ranked non-agricultural groups and persons taking to agriculture in the districts of Yavatmal and Amaravati in Maharashtra. As new entrants into agriculture, members of low-ranked communities are marginalised and face hostility from dominant landed castes. Not only is knowledge not shared by the upper castes with the new entrants but there is often intense competition between agriculturists. This competition among themselves and the fact that the new knowledge gleaned from marketing agencies is often not suitable to the local conditions or the new knowledge has been inadequately understood by these agriculturists has led to disastrous consequences. The details about agriculturists using excess fertilisers and pesticides in their fields and of not knowing how to deal with outbreaks of pests are indicative of this (Farmers' Commission of Experts 2002, Mohanty and Shroff 2004).

In addition, the entry and growth of markets in the life of a community increases the asymmetry of power among members of an agricultural community and that between a community and the market. Successful agriculturists withdraw from the immediate community of production and identifying themselves as 'progressive farmers' they form alliances not with the other agriculturists of their region but with those who have similar economic status. Identifying the bases and impact of agricultural success among the Patidars of Central Gujarat, Rutten (1995) elaborates the ways in which successful agriculturists move away from local politics to village or regional level co-operative politics and from local and sub-jati divisions to upper caste and class solidarity.

Another social dimension that compounds the individualisation of agriculture is that of the fissioning of joint families into nuclear households. Several of the households that experienced a suicide had recently split from larger joint families so as to be able to climb the social and economic ladder (Vasavi 2004; Citizens Report 2005; Mohanty 2005). In such contexts, the head of the household and in most cases a single person bears the burden of having to eke out a satisfactory livelihood. Bearing risks that arise from debts, growing new crops, or ensuring good sale prices are all burdens on a single individual. Many of the reports on suicides highlight this: of the victims having become heads of households, taking to economic strategies on their own, negotiating the demands of the market with little or no support and thereby bearing heavy loads of multiple risks. In their comparative study, Mohanty and Shroff (2004) describe the burden of individualised decision-making. "Most of the victims were independently looking after agricultural operations and expenses thereof. As many as ninety per cent of the deceased farmers had undertaken or resorted to independent farm related decisions. But the farmers of the control group mostly shared the responsibility with other members of family and some of them did not have even direct involvement in agricultural activities." (2004: 7/8). This is also reiterated by the Karnataka Rajya Raitha Sangha report (Shivaramaiah 2007) which also indicates that many of the suicide victims had not shared their concerns and stresses with either members of their families or with others in the village. "The agriculturists who committed suicide did not share their joys and sorrows with their families. When agriculturists are caught in desperate situations that push them to the edge, there are neither family nor institutional based support systems. Either before the suicide or after, there seems to be little support structures" (translated from Shivaramaiah 2007: 23). For the Telengana region, Venkateshwarlu describes how victims had faced tensions within the family: "Compared to the farmers who sustained with the crisis despite serious debt problems, most of the deceased farmers relatively lacked support from their family members, relatives and friends during the crisis. Lack of support from other family members led to tensions within the family, leading to quarrels in certain cases. In some cases the deceased persons were blamed for their mismanagement of family economic affairs and were made responsible for the crisis" (1998: 39).

Independent decisions, made especially in the context of recently nucleated families, place enormous burdens agriculturists who are operating individually and are not part of collective decisions. Each of them faces the burden of large debts, loss of crops and loss of face. All of these: the separation of agriculturists from each other, the loss of a shared body of knowledge and practices, the onerous burden of risks borne by heads of households and enterprising individuals, and the precarious position of new agriculturists can be identified as leading to the individualisation of agriculture.[13] In the individualisation of agriculture lies the disembedding of the shared social and cultural basis of agriculture and the insertion of the individual agriculturist as an 'independent' player into the market economy.

Agricultural individualisation has significance at the cultural and social levels. For one, this is observable in the shifts in conceptualisations of crop loss. Though several regions of India have had long histories of crop loss resulting from drought, pests, rains and floods, records of suicides related to crop loss have been rare. A primary reason for this may have been the extent to which crop loss was configured within a cultural frame that was based on a divinity-nature-human paradigm (see Vasavi 1999). More specially, given the similarities of agricultural patterns within a region, crop losses were collectively experienced phenomena and hence the collective loss was borne as shared trouble. However, the new agricultural pattern privileges individual and independent forms of agriculture where class variations (such as in crop types and kind of agriculture within a region) of agriculture render variations in risks itself. As a result, crop loss, like agricultural production, is an individually borne experience.

But in being constituted as an individual agriculturist, the average marginal agriculturist lacks any substantial support or wherewithal to be a fully prepared and competitive economic player. For one, most members of the household and family are also in most cases in conditions of vulnerability. Any new demand on the marginal household and family economy, without adequate replenishment from additional sources, triggers within it mechanisms of fission and imposes special burdens on the already fragile households.

Agriculture, long embedded with the rural caste system and acting as the key source of reproduction of the caste system, is now the site of economic modernity (bringing with it the individualisation of actors) where it is sought to be altered through the introduction of technology, intensification of its links to the market, and introduction of new knowledge forms. For those economically and socially marginal in the system, the games of the new agricultural modernity and its technologisation induce and induct them into new risks. But the individualised economic actor remains embedded within the social and cultural fabric of her or his society and is therefore circumscribed by its norms and values.

What results is the working of two differing sets of cultural logics,[16] that of the new economic regime that privileges the individual acting for his or her own economic benefit and therefore leads to the individualisation of a person. Yet at the same time, the individual, though permitted to be an independent economic actor, is also expected to subscribe and adhere to the cultural pressures of the social world. As a result, the average marginal agriculturist bears two contradictory burdens; individualised at the economic level and bearing the multiple risks associated with commercial agriculture and at the same time playing out the roles and responsibilities associated with being a compliant and active social player. What Julie Livingston highlights for Botswana, which has also recorded high levels of suicide during a time of economic boom is relevant here: "It is not that social life has atrophied or constricted so much as the relations between self and others have shifted in disorienting ways as consumption and sociality stoke one another" (2009: 675). These pressures are, in turn, enhanced by conditions of declining capability at the household level and a further erosion of possible support structures.

Household Capability Decline

The marginal agricultural household is in the best of circumstances faced with multiple challenges of meeting its own requirements of sustenance and of being able to be engaged in economically viable activities, either through its own independent labour or by combining labour on its land along with the sale of its labour power (working for wages on others' land). In these circumstances, the 'fall-back position' of such households is contingent on their ownership and control of assets, access to employment and income generation, access to common property resources, availability of external social support including credit from kin and informal sources, and support from the State (Agarwal 1997). But without access to many of these supporting structures, most small and marginalised cultivating households exist on borderline conditions; barely breaking even, even at good times, and frequently falling into conditions of penury and erosion.

Details of the economic conditions of victims' households indicate the precarious position and onerous burdens that such households and families bore. In their study of seventy six families where debt-related suicides had taken place in Marathwada, Maharashtra, Karulkar (2006) and his team highlight the following: nearly half of the agriculturists were non-literate (49.4 per cent); were predominantly from the Maratha castes; a majority (58 per cent) were from small and marginal holdings (less than 2 hectares) with about 30 per cent from the medium landholding (2-4 hectares) families. While four per cent of the victims were women, and the average size of the family was 4.6 persons. Seventy-two per cent belonged to the above poverty level families, with average annual expenditure of Rs 36,156, and an average annual income of Rs 13,097; this meant that they had an annual deficit of Rs 23,059. And the average debts of such households at Rs. 1,22,752 was higher than the national average debt for agriculturists (Rs 17,435). Given these conditions of increasing costs of cultivation, growing debt burden, declining capabilities at the household level, and increasing extra costs of living and expenditure, the marginal agriculturist faces fragmentation and erosion at multiple levels.

A key result is the decline in capability at the household and family level. The ability to sustain the family, provision its requirements and meet contingent expenses is eroded. In addition, growing debt burdens pose the problem of constantly depleting any savings or additional income. In such contexts, families experience intense forms of vulnerability which are experienced at multiple levels. Diane Elson's description of the impact of capability decline in the household is apposite here: "When people have to live hand to mouth, human energies and morale are weakened; 'contingent labour' is conducive to 'contingent household' which fragment and disintegrate with costs for the people from those households and for the wider society" (1998: 15). New pressures such as demands for education and health expenditure impose high and economically devastating loads on families. These trends are corroborated by studies such as that by Anirudh Krishna (2008) which indicate that expenditure on health needs alone is the single biggest reason for families to drop back into poverty. Linkages between such expenditures which erode the household's capabilities (to be able to work, save, sustain the family's requirements etc.) are also substantiated by Meeta and Rajiv Lochan's study (2006) of households which reported health and education expenditure as being key causes for suicides in Maharashtra. That capability decline in the household level is a key reason for increasing the vulnerability of marginal agriculturists is observable from comparative data. In the states where the provisioning of basic services, including welfare policies, and linkage to employment serve as the foundation for a minimum safety support system, there are no records of suicides by agriculturists (Vijaybhaskar 2010).

But continuous capability decline, accompanied by intense forms of distress with repeated failure (of crops, inability to settle loans), growing pressures (of children to be married or educated), houses to be built, etc., act as the bases for desperate decisions. Repeated and multiple loans from varied sources, juggling multiple creditors, and seeking support for financial assistance become the game plan of the desperate. What in standard economic analyses seem like poor decisions and excessive risk engagements are really desperate measures of the marginalised and the vulnerable to tide over high levels of distress. The loss of crops from either pests or diseases or the lack of remunerative prices and the inability to repay debts compound the conditions of desperation. Case after case details how victims experienced loss of honour, erosion of self worth and declining social status.

Social Entrapment: New Desires, Debts, and Cultural Load

Indebtedness is not a new cultural or economic category in the lives of most Indians. Hindu scriptural and cultural injunctions see debt or *rna* as constitutive of the personhood of Hindus (Malamoud 1996). Economically, a long history of agricultural indebtedness (Stokes 1972) has marked the lives of most agricultural families and households. Indebtedness is also a significant social act, entering into which involves the negotiations of power, identities and selfhood. Personalised loans, from friends, relatives, neighbours and local elite entail entering into relationships of obligations and pressures. If indebtedness itself is a multiple burden, borne only with the hopes and expectations of crafting a new life, then the failure to repay becomes additionally burdensome. Each reminder and pressure placed on the debtor becomes an infringement of her or his sense of self and honour.

Although all the reports note the extent to which such widespread and high indebtedness among agriculturists was considered by most of the families to be the key reason for the distress experienced by the victims and which led to their suicide,[15] the social impact of such indebtedness and its implications have not been officially or academically recognised. Since the key sources of non-institutional credit have been agri-business agencies (that provide both inputs at deferred credit to agriculturists and also loans), new money lenders, government employees,[16] relatives and friends who draw on their urban salaries, they pose a double burden on agriculturists. For one, interest rates have been exorbitant (ranging from 24 to 45 per cent per annum) and secondly they are linked to their personal and social networks. What is involved in transactions between them are not only economic strategies of typical creditor-debtor relations but also relations of social standing and moral worth.

In addition, the burdens of new agriculture and its multiple risks are not the only pressures on most agriculturists. New aspirations of educating children, growing pressures of socially prescribed consumption, especially in the spheres of rituals and marriages, create serious conflicts in the use of scarce economic resources. Under such conditions, perhaps what is more burdensome is the fact that the individualisation of agriculture is not matched with an individualisation of social and cultural life or with a concomitant individualisation of the private, social sphere. The larger aspirations for upward social mobility, with additional pressures placed by the expansion of the market and the intrusion of the media and its dissemination of consumer desires, have often meant that new lifestyles are marked with consumer goods (Rutten 1995; Breman 2007). Attendant with these trends is the commercialisation of rituals where new goods are added to the list of ritual transactions and a range of new rituals are adopted into the life-cycles of individuals and families. These obligations and pressures leave many an agriculturist with multiple burdens. As most of the cases from the suicide reports highlight, each person bears, in the context of this dual burden of new economic pressures and risks, the social burdens of subscribing to both pre-existing and new collective social obligations. The celebration of life cycle rituals such as the puberty rituals of girls, the conduct of annual *satyanarayan vrat*s, purchase of new goods such as television, bicycles etc., that become part of the symbolic capital of families, have added to the pressures and indebtedness.

Weddings, for long the single biggest source of indebtedness and misery for Indian agriculturists, remains the largest single financial burden on families, and the spread of dowry practices and the increase in the amounts, the types of goods and in the celebration of weddings contribute to new financial burdens. Hence many of the suicides by active, entrepreneurial agriculturists were linked to the expenses they had incurred in getting their children, especially daughters, married. Three of the six cases of suicides by agriculturists that I reviewed in Hassan district of Karnataka were directly related to the onerous debts that the fathers had incurred for providing dowries to their daughters, for the wedding ceremony or to build better houses prior to the wedding. In each case, the debts had increased beyond anticipated levels when crops failed or the prices of their produce had collapsed. And as observed in the report by the Farmers' Commission of Experts (2002) for Andhra Pradesh, the stranglehold of tradition continues even in the post-suicide context where the victims' families feel compelled to spend substantial portions of the compensation, received from the State, on funeral feasts and ceremonies, all obligations and social compulsions which further entrap the victims' families and compound the tragedy.

These diverse and plural social forms of life, where the collective subscription to cultural demands combines with an increasing individualisation within the economic domain and subordinates them to the market and to social entrapment, mark the lives of many marginal cultivators. Berking's observation of this contradiction, "the individualisation of life conduct and the pluralisation of life-forms" (1996: 191) has resonance here. In the larger cultural frame in which economic modernisation is sought along with an intensification of traditionalisation, the individual bears the burden of both worlds; risk and isolation at the economic level, social pressure to prescribe to common desires and expectations, and stigma on the violation of these social norms and standards at the social level. The result is intense stress which is manifested in several ways.

Biographies of Risk

The disengagement and distantiation of individuals from collective networks and the burden on individuals has been elaborated by Beck and Beck-Gernsheim (2001) for the West. They note the increasing individualisation, the separation of individuals from group and collective moorings, and the placing of additional burdens of risk on individuals. This, the processes of disengagement of individuals from collective networks and the stress on the 'do-it-yourself biography' is also relevant in this context of the growing individualisation of agriculture. Compounding established cultural norms of responsibility is the need to handle and resolve problems and challenges on one's own, especially if they are linked to the external world of commercial transactions and to the world of capital.

Richard Swift's description of one of these victims, Bravin Vijay, age 26, of Sunna village in Vidarbha highlights how these risks and burdens were borne at an individual level:

> On 25 November 2006 (Bravin Vijay)...got up early and rode his new (but unpaid-for) motorbike out into the fields and hanged himself from an electrical pole. Bravin was deep in debt to both moneylenders and the co-operative bank. A loan for a well had come up dry. Cotton prices were what they were. He was responsible not only for his new wife but also for his parents and siblings. He was caught between the obligations of old rural India and the desires of shiny new consumer India, as represented by his new motorbike. He must have felt that he could satisfy neither. His father referred to Bravin as a sensitive son who felt that 'all the responsibilities fell on him'. (2007: 6)

What surfaces here about the new agriculturist (marginal in economic and social position and seeking to engage with capital and high technology) are characteristics of what Beck and Beck-Gernsheim describe as being aspects of risk societies, where biographies become a 'do it yourself biography' that is "always a risk biography, indeed a tightrope biography, a state of permanent (partly overt, partly concealed) endangerment" (2001: 3). This is relevant for marginalised agriculturists caught in the web of risks emanating from their own precarious economic and social position and in the unreliability of the new agricultural regime. What Beck and Beck (2001) elucidate as the 'do-it yourself biography' (which) does often become a 'breakdown biography' is visible in the way in which individualised and marginalised agriculturists have borne the new loads of risks. Withdrawn into their individualised households and families, agriculturists are often unable to gauge the risks involved in engaging with an unpredictable market, varying and unreliable climatic conditions, unreliable quality of seeds, fertilisers and pesticides, and unsure and untested forms of new agricultural practices.

Humiliation and the Erosion of Self

Under such conditions the inability to repay loans has ripple effects on the person and his and her family. Acts of demands for repayment, and taunts that meet the person become larger than mere insults. Each of these interactions becomes a form of humiliation which is also intensified when social relations are in conditions of fluidity and marginalised persons are attempting to overcome entrenched forms of discrimination or disadvantage (Palshikar 2010). And in many cases, the humiliation in front of others when they were unable to repay the loans was the last straw that subsequently led to the act of committing suicide. Various reports provide poignant portrayals of such conditions. For the Punjab, Iyer and Manick (2000) describe how Balwinder Singh, a Jat Sikh had borrowed money from the agricultural commission agents and a cloth merchant to purchase and set up a tube-well and fix a pump set in his land of three and a half acres. He had failed to repay the loan on time, as the market prices had not been remunerative, and he had been humiliated in front of others. After a period of restlessness and anxiety, he had consumed pesticides and died. Similarly, in Muddenahally village of Hassan district of Karnataka, I recorded the suicide by an agriculturist, Thammaiah, at the age of fifty five.[17] Known as an enterprising agriculturist, Thammaiah had given up his caste occupation of toddy tapping and had taken to agriculture. He had worked hard to purchase three hectares of land and in the recent years had worked even harder to take to commercial agriculture. The declining water table and the drought in 2003 had laid his fields barren and the sum of rupees one lakh and forty thousand that he had borrowed the previous year at an interest rate of thirty six per cent, to sink a well, had multiplied at compound rates. He had taken more loans for his son's and daughter's weddings and was worried about the lack of production from his fields. Thammaiah had desperately tried to increase his income through sale of *neera*, the liquor from coconut trees, but this was also not as lucrative as he had expected. As his debts piled up and he failed to make payments, the creditors started to visit his home and village. Unable to bear the tension from their periodic visits, Thammaiah, often stayed in the fields and refused to come home regularly. On the morning of 9th September 2003, a neighbour and fellow village-cultivator had found him hanging from a tree in his field.

Encounters between creditors and the indebted create a deep sense of shame among the indebted. Shame here is a result of a loss of public esteem, honour, and self worth. All of these are relational identities and subjectivities which mark individuals in their self constitution. Shame, either constructed by one, or experienced in front of others becomes a diminishment of the self (Taylor 1985). Within the framework of a culture which privileges honour and places an onus on each individual to maintain self-worth and 'face' are narratives that indicate what triggered the drastic resort to suicide. Most of the victims, who were in their own ways entrepreneurs and initiators, had faced a deep sense of disappointment, a social fall in their standing and the potential to have grown economically and socially, loss of crops and the subsequent conditions of penury and/or the loss of face in being accosted or exposed as a defaulting debtor. Family members, mostly wives and older children, narrate the state of mind, social relations, and orientation of the victims just before they committed suicide. While the phrase 'depressed' or being depressed' were typically not used,[18] most of the family members or neighbours describe the victim as either spending long hours alone, being preoccupied or upset, or crying when looking at the crops. In

Mandya district (Karnataka), Savitramma described to me how her friend, Chanamma, a woman past her sixties who had hung herself at home, had spent the previous two weeks looking desolate and was uncommunicative.[19] She had received a second notice from the bank to repay her outstanding loans. To repay her debts she had sold one acre of the family land and had only another acre left. As a widow who had sought to make a better life for her family, and had struggled alone to undertake new cultivation on her land, the new notice from the bank had completely destroyed her. "She used to sit near the field and not do anything". "She had stopped talking to us and did not join us for lunch in the fields", her childhood friend and cousin told me.

Aparna Pallavi's description of her interaction and interview with Chandrakala Meshram, widow of Gangaram, a Gond[20] who had committed suicide in a village in Yavatmal district, Maharashtra, captures this sense of deep loss, shame, and desperation that he must have experienced. As the widow describes, Gangaram had "stopped telling me anything. Where money was coming from, who he was borrowing from, what the crop was like. He was not like that earlier". Further, "He used to look tired more often. He was brooding. I had never seen him that way before" (Pallavi 2006:43-44).

The sense of diminishment[21] of the self is experienced in the context of this agricultural loss, the let down in the face of raised expectations, and the loss of hopes pinned on the crops that would have high market value and make possible a better life. The inversion of all this – the failure of the crops, the inability to get adequate market prices, the inability to repay debts – become loads on the much invested agriculturist, leading to both deep disappointment and diminishment. In their commentaries on the life of the victims, many village residents noted the conditions and empathised with the loss of social standing of the victims. "He felt small", "was concerned about the loans", "he felt that he had wasted his labour", "did not have the stomach for such dishonour", "a hard working woman who only wanted the best for her family and was always very upright", were some descriptions of the victims.

Shame as the social emotion that arises from the monitoring of one's own actions by viewing oneself from the standpoint of others (Fullagar 2003) places the burden of humiliation on those who have ventured to enhance the well-being of families, only to leave them worse-off or to expose them to degradation that they had not known. Here shame emanates not from a simple reproduction of a 'culture of shame' or a 'culture of honour' with its strict codes of conduct and principles of adherence to norms and rules. Rather, shame is here a result of the excessive burden that each victim had borne in their venture into new individualised economic enterprises. Hence, what we are witness to is the working not of a typical 'shame-culture' with its honour code and consequent demands on the individual, but the manifestations of the fall-out of the new and excessive forms of 'competitive individualism', which as Kathryn Dudley has elucidated for the United States results from intense competition among agriculturists as they face expanding capital and the vagaries of international markets (Dudley 2002: 187). The results become more evident "when economic dislocation erodes the institutional infrastructure that organises a particular way of life, (and) a cultural system can be stretched to the limits of coherence and its underlying contradictions revealed" (Dudley 2002: 187).

Details about the victims from the reports and my own observations from six villages indicate that the suicides, when linked to agricultural loss and distress, were acts that combined elements of desperation, humiliation and loss of self. As desperate acts undertaken to escape the situation of humiliation, the suicides were therefore attempts to both overcome the situation and call attention to the larger problem, of which she or he was only one player or victim. In each case of suicide the overall vulnerable situation of the household, falling into penury or destitution, the slippage from high aspirations and expectation, and the unbearable burden of futile efforts acted as triggers to their desperate act.

Cultural Scripts and Legitimisation of Suicides

Several villages in Maharashtra, Punjab, Karnataka and Andhra Pradesh have reported multiple suicides in single villages and multiple suicides in the same family. In gaining 'epidemic' levels, in as much as the suicides intensified in particular areas and villages, and have become part of the discourse on agriculture-related distress and despondency, they have also been abetted by the social sanction and cultural legitimisation they received. While some popular reports and a few select 'expert' committee reports also sought to see these suicides as opportunistic ones made with an eye on gaining compensation from the government and/or from excessive media attention, it would be more accurate to see how the suicides were culturally constructed by persons in the vicinity of these victims. As reports have elaborated and from what I have gathered during field visits, the suicides at the heights of the periods of agricultural loss and enormous economic slippages, were seen not as violations of either cultural codes of the ethics of sustaining life, or that of violating formal and legal codes of conduct, but as acts that flagged the distress of the communities and were therefore public acts to be recognised as such by others. Overarching each of these desperate acts, especially in contexts where the suicides gained intensity and spread in specific regions, were the broader cultural scripts by which every suicide was located into a discursive narrative in which people considered the lives of all agriculturists to be precarious, "not worth living" and "not seen by the big powers who rule" them. Most suicides, of men, old and young, of women as heads of households, were legitimised and accepted not as 'abnormal', anti-social acts, as suicides typically are. Instead the suicides were constructed as acts that one could empathise with and as signs of the larger problem which all members of the village experience. Funeral feasts, ritual feasts on the thirteenth day of death, photographs that are garlanded and displayed prominently in homes of the victims, and the narratives that accompany reconstructions of the life and struggles of the victims indicate how suicides have become normalised and culturally legitimised.

What many reporters and scholars have cited as odd, illogical, and uneconomic actions, such as celebrating the funerary rituals of the suicide victim in a grand way, even using large portions of the compensation amounts or getting into fresh loans, for such funeral feasts in honour of the dead, are acts that signal the cultural acceptance of such deaths. In some cases, village residents have come together to collect funds to contribute to the funeral rites and feasts conducted for the memory of the person. The very collective acceptance of such suicides has then acted as a form of cultural legitimisation of the suicides thereby signalling the extent to which each death was seen as an act to call attention to the degraded conditions of the agricultural collective.

Despondency and desperation mark the commentary of most agriculturists. As they witness these suicides in their neighbourhoods and villages and as news spreads from one village to the other, their degraded conditions, the helplessness of people, the onerous burdens of agriculture and of being agriculturists are reinforced. "We agriculturists are always in the dark", Savitramma tells me as we prepare to leave her house in a village in Mandya district, Karnataka.

Suicides by agriculturists are therefore a result of the combination of a crises of production and livelihood and compounded by an experience of social estrangement. In their attempts to enhance their livelihoods/agricultural production and their socio-economic conditions, marginal agriculturists take to commercial agriculture. Entrapped in a web of risks (of vagaries of the market and ecology; uncertainty of knowledge and lack of support) agriculturists lose their sense of agency and fortitude, and suicide is seen as the only way out.

What most newspaper reports and many official reports have not recognised – that it is not the individual alone (as weak, failing and inept) but the larger structural bases of the distress (of failing agriculture, the humiliation of loss and debt, the burdens of multiple onerous responsibilities and demands) that leads to 'suicide' – is recognised by members of the agrarian communities. In some cases, suicides in the village have been seen and represented as a social issue, a loss felt and expressed by all.[22] In their ritualisation of suicides, violating established religious proscription of regular funeral rites to persons who commit suicides, they seek to recognise the pain and sacrifice of those who have died and in their own way they erase the official constructions of the victims as 'sick', as legal 'violators' and of the agrarian crises as a non-issue. That official non-recognition of the links between these suicides that they construct as 'sickness' or 'weakness' and of the larger crises is also part of the making of the new 'global risk society' is elaborated by Ulrich Beck; "Social crises appear as individual crises, which are no longer (or are only very indirectly) perceived in terms of their rootedness in the social realm" (1992: 100).

The suicides and their legitimisation in the rural communities and their views and expressions of desperation are not merely products of the decelerating agricultural economy or of the frustrations of being caught in cycles of indebtedness or of being thwarted in their attempts to improve their economic and social well-being. Compounding their conditions of desperation are the attitudes, policies, and responses of the government, the political parties and the wider national social institutions which address the rural and agriculture in demeaning terms and which contribute to further enhancing their marginal condition. Rural India in general and many of the more marginalised ruralities in particular have been subject to processes of marginalisation by the State and what has resulted is the enhanced marginality of the rural as a site, an economy, and of all its residents as citizens. In the overall marginality of the rural lie the reasons for why there has not been any significant mobilisation against what is an unprecedented tragedy: suicides by large numbers of agriculturists.

Notes

1 The case studies of families and households of victims from the various states were compiled by reviewing them for details pertaining to the following criteria: size of cultivation unit, relationship to the land (owner, tenant), caste, use of labour, type of crop/s grown, method of cultivation, production problems, access to capital, indebtedness, source of indebtedness, interest rates and modes of repayment, personal and/or family problems; immediate trigger for distress; compensation received or not.

Each of the reports uses different measurements (hectares or acres), although the Indian standard measurement of land is hectares. Converting acres into hectares (2.5 acres = 1 hectare), I have standarised the landholding patterns from all the reports to arrive at the comparative picture, but in the description I have retained the measurements as indicated by the different reports.

2 The 'Backward Classes' refers to the official identification of those caste groups who are not from the Scheduled communities (castes and tribes) and as those also experiencing social and economic disadvantages. Identification of such groups is done through commissions set up by various states and the criteria often vary, although economic, social, educational and political disadvantage are considered key. In most cases, those identified as 'Backward Classes' come from the non-cultivating caste groups and are predominantly former pastoralists, and a wide range of artisan and service caste groups.

3 The 'Other Backward Classes' (OBCs)refers to further official identification of disadvantaged caste groups to include those not recognised in either the Scheduled Communities list or that of the Backward Classes list. Although identification and official recognition are contentious, in most cases, the OBC are represented by groups such as

itinerant workers and special service caste groups. The term 'Denotified Tribes' refers to those once notified by British colonial policy as 'robbers', 'killers' etc., who are now officially denotified.

4 The Experts Committee Report for Karnataka (GoK 2002) and the studies on Kerala do not indicate the caste background of the victims.

5 Several studies note the increasing pauperisation and displacement of small and medium cultivators. For some recent studies see Rao (2001), Rao (2005), Patnaik (2003, 2004).

6 Case studies of victims' families are available in the reports for Punjab, Andhra Pradesh, Karnataka, and Maharashtra.

7 While Mohanty and Shroff (2004) provide interesting comparative details for the households, they seem to give more weightage to 'social problems' than to distress caused by economic conditions especially of the stress caused by defaulting on loans as key reasons for the victims to have resorted to suicide.

8 Here I draw on Chayanov's idea of the 'self-exploitation' of peasantry or petty commodity producers. For an updated elaboration of Chayanov's theory and its contemporary relevance see the comprehensive essays by Henry Bernstein (2009) and Theodor Shanin (2009).

9 By emphasizing the cultural and not only the social structural changes in rural, agrarian structures I do not overlook the extent to which the social structural basis, drawn on the caste based allocation of resources, is largely intact. Cultural changes are primarily in the arena of forms of practices of agriculture, and the meaning and significance of agricultural activities, gender relations and status, and the new consumer culture and neo-traditionalisation linked primarily to sanskritisation.

10 Both, Paul Richard's (1993) observation that agriculture is 'performed' in the typical non-commercial context and also 'planned' (Waterbury 1996) are valid in the Indian context. In many cases, agriculture was a combination of the performance that draws on the cultural idioms, symbols, and social network and was also planned as agriculturists sought to integrate the new knowledge system and the new networks that were emerging with the market.

11 See my work on agricultural land use and classification (Vasavi 1999).

12 Sociological and recently even economic literature has stressed the

fact that there has been a retention of agrarian structures that lead to a coinciding of caste and class structures in rural India (see Harriss-White 2003).

13 I first used the phrase, 'individualisation of agriculture', in 1999 after a review of the suicides by agriculturists in Bidar (see Vasavi 1999). As I elaborated in other essays that followed (Vasavi 2009), I was unaware of the specific usage of the term 'individualisation' by Ulrich Beck and Elizabeth Beck-Gernsheim and now note that it was used in 2002 (first in the year 2001 (in German) and in 2002 in the English edition). In an interview in the same book, Ulrich Beck qualifies the meaning of individualisation by noting that it refers to "the transformation of work; the decline of public authority and increasing personal isolation; a greater emphasis on individuality and self-reliance…." (p. 202). He goes on to note that individualisation encapsulates "the sociological transformation of social institutions and the relationship of the individual to society." (p. 202). While much of this is with reference to the West and its phase of second modernity, I note the relevance of some of this in the context of the commercialisation of agriculture and the entry of the neo-liberal market in rural India.

14 I draw on the term, 'cultural logics' as used by Aihwa Ong (1999) to describe cultural factors or reasons invoked by actors in both economic and political contexts.

15 The debts themselves were for two primary reasons; predominantly that of supporting agricultural production costs and in some cases for social purposes or what some reports have identified as debts for 'non-productive' expenditures. In Andhra and Maharashtra most loans were taken for production purposes. In Karnataka and Punjab loans were often combined for both production and social purposes, including personal loans for marriages and house construction (Vasavi 2003; GOK/Experts' Committee Report 2002). The IDC report (1998) for Punjab considers non-productive loans to be significant and links such loans with the growth of consumerism. Loans for weddings, houses and consumer goods were the leading reasons for indebtedness. However, other studies such as that by Gill and Singh (2006) refute this and reiterate the centrality of loans for production purposes.

16 The second source of credit in the rural areas, largely undocumented in most of the recent surveys and studies, is linked to the presence of a number of urban employed persons. Those who are residents of villages

and are employed, such as government personnel in the departments of agriculture, electricity, education etc. have sources and levels of income that are not only regular but also high in comparison to average rural income. Such income, including remittances from urban areas, are new sources of usury in the rural areas.

17 From a field study conducted in 2004 in Hassan and Mandya districts of Karnataka.

18 Zachariah (2010) who has studied cases of suicides of those consuming pesticides in the Kaniyambadi block in Tamil Nadu observes that "most of the cases were impulsive and only 22 per cent had underlying depression" (2010: 177).

19 Field Notes on Agrarian Distress; Karnataka, March-June 2004 (Vasavi 2004).

20 Gonds are classified as tribal or adivasi and are not typically associated with settled agriculture. However, recent trends in the plains indicate the taking to agriculture, including that of commercial agriculture, by some members of tribal groups.

21 There is extensive literature in psychology that explores the concept of 'diminishment'. I have not drawn on this concept or its related literature and have focused on rendering the local words of 'being made small', 'feeling small' etc. as that of a general cultural and social meaning of diminishment and closer to the idea of loss of self.

22 See descriptions of funeral rites of suicide victims for Vidarbha in reports by Sainath (2009; 2010).

Ar ki bachbo? Kemon karei ba bachbo?" [Will we live? How on earth will we live?]

Woman protester recuperating in a hospital after being assaulted by the police, Nandigram, West Bengal, 2006

To be declared redundant means to have been disposed off because of being disposable – just like the empty and non-refundable plastic bottle or once-used syringe...

Zygmunt Bauman, *Wasted Lives*, 2004

Chapter Five

Retrogression of the Rural

The modern sector expanded but the dualism refused to go away. The discourse sought to cope with this persistence of underdevelopment in terms of myriad of strategies and techniques of governmentality.
Kalyan Sanyal, *Rethinking Capitalist Development*, 2008

News, Commission reports, fact-finding reports, depositions by agriculturists in 'public hearing' sessions, and a number of studies continue to be made around the issue of 'farmers' suicides'. Located within the shadow space in which suicides are counter and antithetical to the narratives of the 'new' and global India, the suicides in the agricultural belts continue to be treated by the dominant society with skepticism and insensitivity. Government response has been to largely promulgate piece-meal programmes that address only some of the symptoms of the distress and not its real structural bases. Despite the deployment of two large monetary 'packages' to relieve agriculturists' debts and to provide employment to the poor and marginal, the suicides have continued. Most families of the victims have not received any compensation and many have been rendered into conditions of destitution and desperation (Sainath 2010). Widows and dependent children continue to bear the burden of inherited and growing loans and in many cases forms of debt bondage continue (Hardikar 2009). Follow-up reports by Aparna Pallavi (2007) and Ranjana Padhi (2009) highlight the further degradation of families of the suicide victims: widows face contestations over land rights from male members of extended families; are subject to displacement from landholdings or are forced to resort to manual work to sustain themselves and their children; children are withdrawn from school so as to supplement family income; the rights to compensation for victims' families are contested and/or delayed by an insensitive bureaucracy.

Saving Agriculturists from Suicides

Far from seeing and addressing the problem of such large-scale suicides as a structural problem that requires immediate systemic solutions and alterations, the government, especially the state governments have sought to blame the agriculturists themselves. In fact, many state governments have attempted to understand the spate of suicides as a sign of personal weakness among agriculturists or indicative of their dependency. Evidence of such a perspective is available from the Government of Karnataka's (2002) terms of reference to the Experts' Committee which was expected to not only enquire into the reasons for the high numbers of suicides among agriculturists but to also 'identify and recommend measures or programmes to instil self-respect (*swabhimana*) and self-reliance (*swavalamban*) among farmers' (2002: 2). The Maharashtra government sought the help of popular, 'hugging guru', Mata Amritanandamayi, and other spiritual leaders to assist in addressing the crisis in the Vidarbha region and to set up spiritual guidance and rehabilitation centres.[1]

The National Policy for Farmers identified 'distress hotspots' (GoI 2006: 39) in the agricultural belts and recommended a range of solutions to alleviate the distress. And the report (GoI 2007) of the 'Expert Group on Agricultural Indebtedness', a committee set up to enquire into the reasons for the suicides and the indebtedness, recognised the systemic nature of the crisis and made a distinction between the agricultural (related to agriculture) crisis and the agrarian (related to the cultivators) crisis. NABARD,[2] the lead bank for agricultural development in the country, set up an 'Action Plan to Address Agrarian Distress in India' and its members, which included Swiss and British experts representing donor bodies, suggested short and long-term management solutions to the crisis (NABARD 2008). While indebtedness was recognised as a key problem, the interlinkages and foundational reasons for such levels and spread of indebtedness, or the multiple risks which confront most agriculturists, were often not recognised. The focus was primarily on alleviating the symptoms of the distress, and the rate of suicides which were to be halted through certain measures that sought to address the symptoms and not the causes for such suicides.

The oversight of the structural and systemic deficits and problems that have led to the suicides and the failure to deploy appropriate systemic measures have been the key reason for the failure of the 'relief packages' to have provided relief or to have stemmed the suicides. The deployment of monetary relief packages,[3] part of the political strategies of appeasing the rural electorate, did not in of themselves resolve the situation or alleviate the problems of agriculturists in general or that of the most vulnerable, the marginal cultivators. An audit of these packages by the office of the Comptroller and Auditor General (CAG) highlighted that not only were there problems in the implementation of the packages but that there were problems in conceptualisation and inconsistent with local needs. Not surprisingly then, the money did not help mitigate the gargantuan agrarian crisis or even reduce farmers' suicides. The report acknowledges, "Farmers' suicides shot up dramatically even when the two packages were in vogue." One of the important deficiencies that the CAG audit found was the fact that the funds spent did not improve agricultural support prices. In the CAG's summary, it was pointed out that "... agrarian distress essentially caused by unremunerative agriculture would start rising again in the closing years of the package (2008-09)" (cited in

Hardikar 2008). As criticisms of the packages, especially of the debt moratorium packages, have highlighted, the non-recognition of informal credit agencies, the oversight of the production conditions and risks faced by marginal agriculturists etc. have meant that much of the funds supposedly reserved for vulnerable agriculturists have not reached them.

The Commission for Farmers' Welfare, instituted by the Andhra Pradesh government in 2004, to enquire into the large number of suicides by farmers in Andhra Pradesh was more specific in identifying the causes for the distress. In their report, the Commission members noted the failure of public policy which had "systematically reduced the protection afforded to farmers and exposed them to market volatility and private profiteering without adequate regulation, reduced critical forms of public expenditure, destroyed important public institutions and did not adequately generate other non-agricultural economic activities" (Commission for Farmers' Welfare 2005: 7-8).

Distancing the rural from the popular imaginary of the 'new India', media and government reports seek to address the rural, the agriculturist, and agriculture as objects that are either redundant or as aberrations to the new national economy. The rural and the agricultural are represented as problems, existing in a time and space warp that is antithetical to the larger design and desire of a globalizing India. Most reports overlook the details, the variations in their conditions and the complex factors which have rendered the rural into sites of distress and seek primarily economic solutions to a mega problem that is layered and complex.

The government's oversight of such a large-scale and persistent form of agrarian distress as manifested in the suicides is evident in the comparison with how it handled another 'crisis' in the economy; that of the possible collapse of one of the Information Technology(IT) industries. On January 7th, 2009, the Chairman and owner of Satyam

Computers, one of the largest IT companies in India and employing around fifty-two thousand people, confessed to having doctored the company's accounts and of feeling that he was "riding a tiger not knowing how to get off without being eaten".[4] As the company swerved on the brink of bankruptcy, and with imminent threats of withdrawal from Western, multinational clients, the Government of India stepped in.[5] By January 10th, within three days of this announcement, the company's law board was reconstituted and on the 11th of January, three eminent national persons were appointed to oversee a change of hands. Balking at a complete bailout, so as to sustain the IT industry itself, the government then permitted Satyam computers to be bought out by another private company. And within a span of a few months, the crisis seemed to have blown over. Although the scam of manipulated and false accounts was compared to the Enron case,[6] the government's handling of the failure of this large company saw no loss of jobs in the company itself or in the IT sector, no dent in the reputation and viability of India's IT industry, and the overall environment and celebration of IT as the flagship industry of the new global economy continued uninterrupted.

In contrast to the speed, expertise, and focus deployed to rescue one IT company, issues related to the rural and the agricultural continue to face delayed, partial and lackadaisical responses. Such a neglect, that is broadly social, and emphatically economic, and partially political, accounts for the reason that so significant a problem as the large number of suicides by agriculturists continues to be represented and seen as an aberrant case in the otherwise positive economic climate of the nation. The decline of the rural was visible in the year 1997 itself. As the nation celebrated fifty years of independence, as the sparks of the new, global economy, and the newly ascendant economic growth path were being recognised, the rural was already placed in the backseat. In the new imaginaries and expectations of the nation, agriculture was not the future. What was rural and/or agrarian were not fashionable issues to be reviewed. Even a comprehensive and insightful portrayal of the nation such as Khilnani's, *The Idea of India* (1997), which marked and took stock of the nation after half a century of independence, made no mention of how the rural and the agricultural had been altered over the years. To unpack what accounts for this 'moral blindness' (Bauman 2001:253) to this pressing and urgent issue one must locate the multiple ways and levels by which the rural, the agricultural, and agriculturists have been experiencing forms of retrogression from the larger nation.

The Rural as 'Anti-Economy'

Since 1997, the responses of the State and its bureaucracies, politicians, star corporate leaders, and several new entrepreneurs have focused on the making of a 'global India', a 'new' and potentially superpower India. Subsequently, the rural, in general, receded from the imaginary of the key economic and political forces. Major policy documents and budgetary allocation focused on the urban and the global economy. The most glaring fact to indicate that the rural as a sector and agriculture as an economy continue to be neglected is evident in that national budgetary allocation for agriculture has been on the slide downwards. Since the fourth plan (1966-69) outlay of 31 per cent for agriculture, there has been a steady decrease resulting in a mere 10.6 per cent outlay in the tenth plan (2002-2007). Between the period of 2004-2009, the most intense period of the agrarian distress and recording the highest levels of suicide, the average allocation for agriculture was only 0.18 per cent of the total budget (Reddy and Mishra 2009).

Since the late 1990s, most of the states have been encouraged to produce 'Vision Documents' charting terms and trends for the long-term economic future of their regions. Such exercises, conducted under the aegis of state departments of planning, but often worked on by independent consultants and without any or much public consultation, have sought to reduce the population in agriculture as an inevitable trend in national development and have provided financial, policy, procedural, subsidies and other support to urban areas and economies to facilitate this transition.[7] National level documents and books such as those by the former President, A.P.J. Abdul Kalam (1998) and a former IIT director, P.V. Indiresan (2003) represent such perspectives. Both repose faith in the continuity of the new high[8] economic growth rates, invoke the abilities of high technology to solve problems of poverty, and consider social engineering via good governance and the technological management of the masses to be the panacea for most ills of the nation. Documents for both Andhra Pradesh and Karnataka, as also for several other states, prescribe the shifting of the large masses of agriculturists towards more efficient livelihoods, suggest the commercialisation of agriculture to make it both competitive and efficient in the global market, envisage a stronger economy based on the increasing of volume of people in services, and endorse ideas that technology and appropriate management of resources will solve all the structural problems of poverty.

Such strategies and discourses have only further legitimised the role of the market with an emphasis on entrepreneurship and productivity rather than on sustainable agriculture, distribution, and equity. Subsequently, the focus on the market and the individual makes it all the more legitimate to lay the blame for failure on individual agriculturists. What has coalesced together in the period between 1997-2010, even as the death toll by suicides has risen, is the production of a retrogression of all that is rural: the rural as a site, agriculture and allied livelihood forms as economic activities, and agriculturists as economic actors and as citizens.

In the disregard for rural society and economy, the government, corporate leaders and the media have overlooked the specificities and complexities of agriculture and its linkages to the larger well-being of the majority of the people and have rendered the rural into a space called the 'anti-economy'. As Cameron and Palan elucidate, such an 'anti-economy' is forged on the anvil of "imagined economies of globalisation" which is "an auxiliary imagined realm made largely of spatial pockets located in the 'Third World', the countryside and the 'inner cities' and inhabited by the poor and the unemployed" (2004: 131). Such an 'anti-economy', does not consist only of a physical marking off from the national economy, or of being marked as a marginal space. But, the rural as an 'anti-economy' is labelled as being an out-dated economy, and "consigned to a residual space as remnants of older, obsolete norms of economic participation" (Cameron and Palan 2004: 131). That this relegation of the rural and the agricultural is part of the international regime of development is evident from the body of policy documents that institutions such as the World Bank and the Asian Development Bank have disseminated. Reports such as World Development Report/*Agriculture for Development* (World Bank 2008) see agriculture in Asia as a laggard that needs to be replaced and the population as requiring shifts to the more dynamic urban, global economy.

It is the rendering of the rural and the agricultural as an 'anti-economy' that largely accounts for the relegation of the information of the suicides into a 'shadow space' which then legitimises the way in which the distress of the suicides and the problems themselves are sought to be ignored or dealt with partial and ineffective measures by the government.

Rural Forbearance

Conditions at the level of the rural areas and the villages are also responsible for the failure of rural society and polity to be able to handle the onset of the distress. That the distress has been ongoing for more than a decade (1997-2010) and yet no forms of large scale protests, movements or rebellions have gathered force have become an issue. This contrasts with historical evidence wherein indebted agriculturists had often mobilised to demand debt moratorium or had voted with their feet by large-scale abandonment of agriculture or the villages (Stokes 1978). Contrary to this, the contemporary scenario has witnessed agriculturists committing suicide in large numbers.

Two factors account for the lack of political will to address the problems through either initiating structural changes or in ensuring relevant and successful programmes and schemes to alleviate the distress. The first factor relates to the complexity of political conditions in the rural areas and the other to the failure of agriculturists to mobilise themselves and engage in collective actions. A key reason for increasing politicisation but lack of mobilisation may be linked to trends in the very structuring and impact of decentralised democracy and the compulsions of the new economy.

A key objective of the revamped structure of decentralisation of administration (through the 73rd Constitutional Amendment) was to enable the delivery of development programmes to the grassroots. But in reality in most states genuine devolution of power to the decentralised bodies is yet to be fully realised. As one reviewer notes, "...devolution in this respect is hardly taking place. Majority of the state governments have given only soft powers to the panchayats with regard to primary education like providing land, monitoring attendance of teachers without the authority to take action etc." (Tandon 2002: 19). As a result, in many cases, the structures of decentralised administration exist without teeth and the key objectives of enabling local accountability, facilitating development, and enhancing community administration remain distant (Rao 2005). Increasing politicisation of decentralised administration, especially in those states that have actually implemented the new structures, has further fragmented rural society and despite the emergence of members of low-ranked caste groups as key players in the new political field, the agrarian problems and the attendant economic, ecological and social crises remain un-addressed. Such politicisation and fragmentation have compounded the problems of public service programmes and institutions that continue to deteriorate (Vaidyanathan 2006; Reddy and Mishra 2009). Dev (2004) and Sarma (2004) highlight how most government programmes that seek to provision the poor with either foodgrains, housing or employment are also subject to rent-seeking behaviour which in the form of commissions, bribes and misallocation mean that the benefits barely reach the most deserving. Since democracy, and its manifestation at the level of village administration, accountability, transparency and delivery mechanisms have neither deepened nor taken roots in large tracts of the nation's ruralities, the first casualty are the welfare programmes meant for the most marginalised and disadvantaged. In such a context, the deployment of numerous and fragmented welfare programmes ranging from housing, toilets, supplementary food for children to those targeted as 'relief packages' for indebted agriculturists, have only compounded the gains made by middle persons and development entrepreneurs. The inability of most rural settlements and citizens to demand accountability from local leaders and the bureaucracy (Ruud 2000) and to gain access and benefits from the range of development programmes, including special packages such as those of the debt moratorium or relief for alleviating economic distress, is a direct result of this.

The post 1991 period has witnessed a dual and interlinked process in rural India. Even as the volume of marginal cultivators has grown (that is, holdings of less than 2 hectares of land account for 81.3per cent of all landholdings),[9] agriculturists as citizens and agriculture as a subject and economy in general have also been increasingly marginalised in the public sphere and policies of the nation. No longer is even the lip service of 'farmers are the backbone of the economy', or 'the village is the microcosm of India' being made. The inability of the central and state governments, once considered 'an embodiment' of development and 'an engine of agricultural progress' (Ludden 1992: 273), to have reviewed the situation in a comprehensive manner and to have adequately addressed the problems linked to the recurring suicides testify to the marginal position that agriculturists now occupy in the nation's social sensibilities and political economy. Despite widespread criticisms of the Agriculture Minister, Sharad Pawar, and his lack of engagement and contribution to agricultural development, the pressures of competitive electoral politics in the time of coalition politics has meant that he has been retained (post the general elections of 2009) for a second term as Agriculture Minister. What this clearly indicates is the extent to which the state continues to work through its "non-caring policy regime" which "remains deaf to the crisis knocking at the door" (Rao and Gopallappa 2004: 5598).

Policy Gaps and the Erosion of National Agriculture

Agricultural policies since 1991 seem to be on three parallel tracks. One track consists of a body of policies, missions, committee reports, position papers, etc., written by eminent scientists, scholars, and/or science-administrators as heads of committees and organisations. Many of these provide comprehensive reviews and recommendations to scaffold agricultural growth and the rural economy in general. On the second track are a body of policies, or legislations and programmes formulated behind closed doors, without due process or public inputs, which seek to integrate land and agriculture into the larger global neo-liberal economy. While the body of policies of the first track remains largely at the level of rhetoric and rarely sees any realisation into actual programmes, the second track of policies and programmes are finalised by a chosen few and then granted legitimacy through implementation. For example, the policies on Special Economic Zones (SEZs) and the range of new collaborations on the agricultural front have not been subject to widespread debate or scrutiny. US-led programmes such as the secretly concluded and controversial Indo-US deal on agriculture and the Agriculture Biotechnology Support Project (both I and II) funded by the United States Agency for International Development (USAID), led by Cornell University, and implemented in India through the Department of Biotechnology, are examples of the track II policies that not only bypass democratic processes but are also against the interests of small and marginal agriculturists and the sustainability of Indian agriculture.

A third track of agricultural policies are devised at the state level, which overlook policies and stipulations at the central level and primarily comprise of regional populist measures. Provisioning of free electricity has gained popularity even at a time when neo-liberal policies stipulate withdrawal from such subsidies. Subsequently such populist policies defy both economic rationale and environmental safeguards (Balakrishnan et al. 2008) and those who do gain are large farmers and the new entrepreneurial agriculturists and/or the agri-business industries while the decline in public provisioning of key infrastructure and access to credit fall as additional burdens on marginal and small agriculturists (Guruswamy et al. 2008).

In addition to the oversight of economic and social structural factors that are largely responsible for the distress in the countryside, there is an abiding faith in new administrative expertocracy as being able to resolve the problems. For example, the Report of the Expert Group recommends a 'Farmers Livelihood Improvement Mission' (FLIM) at the state and district levels headed by the Chief Minister and the District Collector respectively. "The Mission should be supported by a Livelihood Support Centre (LSC) having professional expertise and manpower to organise the farmers, identify economic opportunities for the farmers, particularly for small and marginal farmers, and create projects and systems in coordination with different stakeholders. The central and state governments, the commercial banks, and other public institutions should play a pro-active role in promoting them." (GoI 2007: 22).

In recommending new and external sources of expertise and new forms of livelihood, towards which agriculturists must be guided, the report represents its authoritative voice and therefore the "gradual establishment of a new structure of domination – the rule of the knowledgeable and knowledge as the ruling force" (Bauman 2001: 112). Having erased much of the local knowledge forms, and continuously overlooking the economic, social, and political structures by which the multiple risks of an agricultural economy and society are reproduced, the report presents a forward looking recommendation that will only build on the existing structures of disadvantage among the majority of agriculturists. Several policies also have a high-technology and market bias in-built into them. Many recent recommendations focus on facilitating and providing remote sensing agencies, information technology, national commodities exchange, insurance provisioning and export outlets etc.[10]

What are consistently overlooked are the problems in the lack of resources (land, water, capital, networks of information and support), problems in knowledge dissonance, the multiple forms and levels of risks faced by most agriculturists and the overall disabling economic environment. These policies and programmes continue despite the fact that the major government report on the agrarian crisis observes that, "The most serious aspect of the crisis in agriculture is deceleration in its growth, and the distressed state of farmers in general, and of small and marginal farmers in particular" (GoI 2007: 2).

Missing from the Media

The oversight and negligence of rural and agricultural issues by the State[11] is compounded by the invisibilisation of rural and agricultural issues by the popular media. Despite the spread, frequency and gravity of the issues, many mainstream media houses fail to provide detailed and continued news and analyses of the suicides. As one critic has pointed out (Arvind 2006), at the height of an epidemic of suicides in Vidarbha in April 2006, much of the media preferred to attend the Lakme Fashion week in Mumbai than report on the emergency situation in the rural areas.

The marginalisation and retrogression of the rural from the collective and dominant imaginaries of the nation is evident from the extent to which even commercial films, considered a repository of popular public sentiment, no longer draw on the rural as the focal site of action. As interests and orientations have moved to the global arena, the diaspora as social stage, consisting primarily of the US and UK, are now the sites and centres of film production. Where the village is shown at all, it is either as a background to the past, a place to which the hero and heroine and their ancestors once belonged, or through the lens of nostalgia that sees the village as the repository of Indian and Hindu civilisation and culture. Rare films, such as that of 'Summer of 2006', which focus on the issues of agrarian suicides and the state of Vidarbha have been unpopular, pulled out of theatres after poor showings. The more recent *Peepli Live* (2010) uses agrarian suicide as a backdrop to critique current political and media constructions and utilisation of the rural but provides no in-depth or insightful perspective of the actual conditions of agriculturists. Critical media attention, if any at all, are now confined to select documentary films that seek to represent some of the trends and concerns but are unable to garner large audiences.

Failure of Agrarian Movements

Despite the voices of a number of organisations that have sought to highlight the plight of the poor and marginalised in various regions,[12] none have had either significant regional presence or national level impact. The inability or failure of agriculturists to mobilise around issues pertinent to agrarian issues and to demand and gain policies that could assure their sustenance and survival indicates a lack of political mobilisation among agriculturists. Not even the populist and publicity garnering agrarian movements such as that of the Karnataka Rajya Raitha Sangha, Shetkari Sanghatana, or the Bharatiya Kisan Union (Gill 2004; Madsen 2001; Suri 2006) have been able to table and enforce a substantial alteration in agricultural policies in order to address such grievances.

Mobilisation, if any, in most rural areas continues to be centred around the interests of the dominant class or upper caste farmers and hence does not often represent the interests of the small and medium agriculturists. Although recently the All India Kisan Sabha, associated with the Communist Party of India (Marxist), has led rallies to address the crisis, a substantial presence of such parties in the rural areas is absent. The CPI (M)'s recent policy stances and support for pro-agricultural and rural programmes including the critique of the UPA government's *Bharat Nirman* indicate growing recognition of the requirements of rural masses. But this stance contradicts the CPI (M)'s own anti-agricultural position and actions in Nandigram and Singur in West Bengal. Such policy formulations and pronouncements indicate shifts in the left parties' engagement with the rural, which, as astutely noted and critiqued by Brass (1995), largely neglected them on the basis of critiquing agriculturists for their fragmented and questionable class identity, and thereby overlooked them as key political actors.

The presence and growth of agri-business and contract farming in some regions also accounts for the coopting of rich agriculturists into industrial agriculture. Assured of quick and high returns, leading agriculturists have submitted to such agendas (Panini 1999) with little or no anticipation of market downturns, loss of genetic diversity, and/or the loss of autonomy. This acceptance of a global agricultural agenda accounts for the reason that the major farmers' movements and groups have not, on the whole, vocally protested the promotion of such policies. Protests and resistance, if any, have more or less risen only in times of crises and loss.

Instead of comprehensive movements to address key issues of structural inequity, a number of fragmented and special interest agrarian movements and organisations have come into being. The recent agrarian movements, especially those since 2000, are not primarily led by agriculturists or constituted by them. Instead, a small and very limited group of people, without party affiliation and drawn from civil rights and democracy movements and organisations, have joined forces with spontaneous movements to fight for land rights and against forced acquisition and conversion of agricultural land into urban and/or industrial lots. P.K. Datta (2008) in his analyses of the mobilisation against forced industrialisation in West Bengal's Singur and Nandigram villages sees these as solidarity movements which contest blatant violations of democratic rights but do not seek to bring about any significant structural transformation.

Some of the forms of recent mobilisation about and for agricultural issues are also reactionary and against the limited attempts to bring about some semblance of equity and justice in the agrarian structure. The Kisan Mahapanchayat in Bihar, composed primarily of landowners, is akin to the Bharatiya Kisan Union of Punjab and Haryana (a stronghold of the dominant landed caste groups) and seeks to contest the possibility of the State initiating a new tenancy law which could provide rights to the large body of sharecroppers and the working poor.[13] The failure to address regional land issues can also be linked to political and economic trends in different regions. As Vijaybhaskar notes for Tamil Nadu, the failure to mobilise against the Special Economic Zones, and overall to issues related to land acquisition is linked to the fact that the state is experiencing "long term crises in agriculture, a process of growing landlessness among marginal farmers, a resultant move towards non-farm employment, a relatively more decentralised pattern of urbanisation and a degree of social mobility among the backward caste..." (2010: 38). The result of such trends has meant the dissipation of all agricultural and rural issues from regional and national political and policy agendas and a constitution of the rural as a populist agenda made with the vote-bank in mind.

The Rural as Vote-Bank

The results of the 2004 parliamentary elections, which saw the routing of the coalition NDA government from power and was read as widespread disaffection against the anti-rural policies and the false representation of a 'shining India', forced the new coalition government to reckon with the rural and the agricultural as powerful vote banks. Subsequently, there has been sudden interest and sympathy for the rural and for the *aam aadmi*, the 'common man' who is now to be reckoned as a voter. That programmes such as the moratorium on agricultural loan debts and the implementation of the Nation Rural Employment Guarantee Programme (now renamed as Mahatma Gandhi National Rural Employment Guarantee Programme) were the bases for the consolidation of the rural vote for the Congress party was evident in the party's victory during the 2009 parliamentary elections.

A new version of the National Commission for Farmers[14] was established in 2006 and it called for a focus on the "economic well-being of the women and men feeding the nation than just on production" (NCF 2006: 3). Yet, details and recommendations made in the report of the Commission indicate the gap between its professed orientation and its support for altering agriculture. Its eight key recommendations focus on further intensifying new knowledge and technology-led forms of agriculture and largely bypass the issue of the majority: that of the lack of access to adequate land and to the complementary set of resources and capital. More glaring is the fact that none of the reports has engaged with a critique of the Green Revolution model, although the suicides and the extant forms of ecological, economic and social distress indicate these to be fall-outs from the model.

Preparing for the General Parliamentary Elections in 2009, the government announced the 'New Deal for Rural India' or the *Bharat Nirman* programme in 2008. Focused on infrastructure development, that is electricity, housing, telephony, roads, water, sanitation and irrigation, this Indian version of the 'New Deal' was in reality an attempt to improve the infrastructure to facilitate market and capital expansion into the countryside. Even as these were presented as substantial government-directed funds and support for the welfare of the majority, the policies in reality supported the industries that gained from the allocation of large-scale funds. Supported primarily by the World Bank and the Asian Development Bank, such programmes facilitated the entry of private construction and service providers, with vested interests unleashing a new reign of violence in the rural areas (Shah 2009). The results of deploying this slew of funds, without the attendant structures and processes, to the legitimate recipients, who are rural residents and agriculturists, has only made issues of development, governance, and democracy all the more complicated. The already fragile structures of decentralised governance have become now further subject to interventions by other parallel structures and agencies; that of the committees and organisations that seek to provision such infrastructure but become powers unto themselves, the rise of agents and entrepreneurs who siphon off large sums allocated to these programmes and the subsequent rendering of the poor and the disadvantaged further into the hands of those with power.[15] The result of these forces largely accounts for the fact that despite large-scale deployment, real and significant impacts on the everyday lives of the rural poor are yet to be realised.

If most of these policies consistently and persistently overlooked the structural bases of inequality in the agrarian structure, the problems in the very model of agriculture being promoted and the enhancement of environmental degradation, they most especially overlooked the very variations in ruralities, the differentiation of agriculturists by land size, ownership of assets, credit etc.

The real success of both these programmes lies in the fact that they have acted as the single-biggest vote collection mechanism and the packages have paved the way for the Congress led alliance, the United Progressive Alliance (UPA), to retain power in the parliamentary elections of 2009. Faced with angry voter dissent and loss of legislative assembly seats and power several political parties deployed populist activities and policies to woo and appease the widespread rural dismay against the predominantly urban focus of most parties and governments. In Karnataka, the Chief Minister, Kumaraswamy, took to 'village stays' (*grama vasthavya*) and efforts were made to represent him as addressing the hitherto neglect of agriculture and as being a friend and supporter of agriculturists. And suddenly the rural poor had again become visible for a short period. Another government voted into power as a backlash against the excessive global economy was that of the Congress-led party in Andhra Pradesh. The new, populist Chief Minister, Y.S.R. Reddy initiated a number of new slogans such as 'The Rural is Right' and programmes such as the 'village square'. That he was to die in a helicopter crash on his way to one of the 'village square' programmes was to render him in the annals of history as a friend of the rural and of farmers and as one who had sought to reverse the depredations of the previous regime's promotion of blind neo-liberal policies. This despite the fact that he promoted policies that intensified land acquisition, displacement of people and unregulated capital intrusion.

The rural as market: discovering those at the 'bottom of the pyramid'

Corporate groups first reacted to the proposed debt moratorium for agriculturists and to the National Rural Employment Guarantee Programme/Act (NREGA) as yet more policies and deployment of funds that were wasted on the rural and the agrarian. Intense criticisms of such wastage of funds and the failure of all governmental programmes to aid the rural and the agricultural sectors and the futility of such interventions formed the core of such criticisms. But, in a dramatic turnabout corporate groups quickly recognised how 'inclusive marketing' could gain profits from the new *mantra* of 'inclusive growth' and the slew of populist packages and programmes. Subsequently, marketing strategies were deployed to capture and capitalise on the new rural consumer who was now the beneficiary of funds aimed at them as rural citizen-voters.

Recognising the sudden availability of consumers in the rural areas, management Gurus now draw on the new slogan,'wealth at the bottom of the pyramid',[16] and marketers, manufacturers, credit agencies and a slew of companies from the very same corporate houses that had objected to budgetary allocations for agriculture and rural areas, suddenly recognise the rural as a market opportunity. Speculators and large industrial houses see rural residents as new consumers and clients, and agriculture as the untapped source of new wealth which needs to be tapped to enlarge the market basis for new production and goods. Such trends are compounded by increased attempts to integrate rural India and those at the 'bottom of the pyramid', as C.K. Prahlad, the internationally renowned management guru called them, into the neo-liberal market. Seeking to tap the market and consumer potential of rural India for a range of goods, such calls fail to recognise the heterogeneity of rural India, and by focusing on only the top-most and economically strong groups attempt to introduce the risks of a consumer society into an already fragmented and fragile context. The new focus on the possible remaking of the rural to fit into the larger economic agenda of a globalised India was also evident when Rahul Gandhi escorted Bill Gates to Amethi, his political constituency. Despite its record for widespread poverty, ill-health, and poor indices of social development, Rahul Gandhi presented a blue-print for the constituency, which with the assistance of Microsoft was to convert Amethi, a predominantly agricultural region, into an Information Technology hub.[17]

The dominance of the logic of the market has meant that the rural poor are increasingly seen as potential consumers rather than as 'exploited producers' (Bauman 2001: 25). The result of this has been that: "With market choice moving simultaneously to the center of self-constitution, societal integration and systemic reproduction, market standards tend to dominate or replace moral responsibilities, and one of the consequences is the dissipation of responsibility for the *distant stranger* – be it contemporary poor, or future generations" (Bauman 2001 : 25). We now see it regularly about rural India; a shifting perspective over the past decade. Once relegated as redundant and a burden, now focused on as a potential market with a sizeable consumer base. The rural has become both, a site for populist palliatives and a target for mass marketing of consumer goods.

Agrarian movements have been unable to address the marginalisation of agriculture as an economy and the relegation of the rights and livelihood options for the rural as citizens. Subsequently, there has been a gathering force of policies and programmes that seek to make the rural redundant or relegated to a position of subordination in the larger economy. The end result of such marginalisation and oversight of the structural problems and deficits of agrarian India has been a series of fallouts – economic, social and ecological, the denouement of which over the years is encapsulated in the current triple crises that several regions of the nation are facing. The overall failure of the State to address these problems has led to the manifestation of these crises in most regions of the nation and in intense forms of distress in some pockets. Two reports, one by the Kashipur Solidarity Group (2008) and the other by the organisation, Vikas Samvaad (2009), describe the conditions of Bundelkhand, a contiguous belt that stretches across parts of Uttar Pradesh and Madhya Pradesh, and which is now manifesting in full blown form the results of the triple crises of ecological, economic and social devastation. Only five hundred kilometres away from Delhi, the Bundelkhand region was once home to a wide variety of agricultural complexes. The promotion of commercial cultivation of crops such as betel leaves, mint, and rice has replaced the earlier crops of millet, wheat, and chick peas. Declining rainfall since 1993 has led to widespread and intense exploitation of ground water through privatised tube and bore wells to support commercial crop cultivation. The deforestation of the surrounding forests, legal and illegal mining activities, and declining public investment in public irrigation systems have meant that most of the rivers and canals have run dry and have compounded the declining agricultural productivity of the region. Lack of land distribution and state support for the labouring poor have left the lower-ranked and working caste groups in conditions of penury, pauperisation and starvation. Large numbers, estimates range from 25-30 lakhs, of people have been forced to migrate from the region and in 2008 the region wore a look of famine-like conditions. Weddings are either postponed or cancelled and families are refusing to marry girls into villages that face acute water scarcity. Several thousand starvation deaths have taken place and some cases of suicides by debt-ridden agriculturists have been reported. Here economic, ecological and social degradation have looped into a circuit where land degradation, declining production, migration and conditions of social distress mark the lives of most people.

India's agrarian distress at the end of the twentieth century and marking the beginning of the new century encapsulates the social, economic and political position of agriculturists in which they remain vulnerable subjects and whose position and rights as citizens are recognised and reckoned with only during elections. Key issues that pertain to them, redistribution of resources, right to basic education, health care and housing, policies that could provide remunerative prices and state support in periods of crises are no longer central to the planning or budgetary agendas, and the official poverty line is increasingly politically determined[18] (Patnaik 2004; Harriss-White 2004). While assessments of poverty levels and the nature of poverty itself have become debatable and contested, the very viability of programmes to address the many poverty-related problems have also become fragmented and contested. In many states the tools, processes, and results of measuring and identifying people as either 'above' or 'below' poverty have become fraught with tension and problems. Matching these have been the limited deployment of welfare measures and the even more limited impact of these on people considered eligible to be declared as 'poor' and therefore worthy of receiving these welfare benefits. Frustration and anger at such governmental neglect has had some unusual responses. In some cases desperate village residents in the Punjab, Andhra Pradesh, and Maharashtra have gone to the extreme of putting up their villages for sale. In Punjab agriculturists have invited the President and Prime Minister of India to conduct a 'human market' for the sale of their kidneys (Sharma 2006: 1).

In the rendering of the rural into conditions of retrogression lie the entrenchment and continuous reproduction of existing structures and conditions of disadvantage of a vast majority of rural citizens. The failure to address rural and agrarian problems has led to the rendering of the urban as increasingly successful and attractive while the rural and the agricultural are rendered into conditions of retrogression and failure. Where long entrenched structures of inequity are sought to be plumped to meet new demands and desires, we are witness to not merely a retrogression of the rural into conditions of economic deceleration and social disarray but into conditions of involution. Herein lies the predicament of rural India – predominantly agricultural by population and occupation, but in a condition where agriculture and agriculturists have been rendered marginal and marginalised in the new economic and social imaginaries of the nation. What the significance and long-term implications of this predicament will be can be gauged by locating the suicides by agriculturists as significant acts that encapsulate the multiple involutions in rural India.

Notes

1 *Deccan Herald*, Sunday, March 18, 2007.

2 National Bank for Agriculture and Rural Development (NABARD) is a Government of India bank and acts as the lead bank for the agricultural sector.

3 In December 2005, the Government of Maharashtra announced a Special Package of Rs. 1,075 crores for six districts of Western Vidarbha. Subsequently, the Prime Minister, Dr. Manmohan Singh, after his visit to parts of Vidarbha in July 2006 announced a comprehensive rehabilitation Package targeted at 31 districts in the four states of Maharashtra, Karnataka, Andhra Pradesh, and Kerala.

4 Cited in his letter (http://www.slideshare.net/guest69d931/satyam-the-letter-that-ramalinga-raju-wrote-reveals-shocking-details-presentation).

5 All details pertinent to the Satyam case are culled from various newspapers.

6 Refers to the 'Enron scandal' in which the transnational energy company went bankrupt after revelations that the audit accounts of the company had been tampered with and misrepresented.

7 Karnataka, Andhra Pradesh, Punjab and Chhattisgarh have vision documents for the periods. In addition to Vision 2020, some of the states, including Karnataka, have 'Vision Plans' for 2050. Although represented as State documents, the work is, typically, assigned to a private group, consultancy or institution and is often representative of corporate interests.

8 Copies of the Vision 2020 documents for Karnataka and Andhra Pradesh are available on the websites.

9 Agricultural Statistics at a Glance, 2008 (GoI), Data refers to 2000-2001 All-India figures; landholding of 0-2 hectares is 81.3 per cent of all holdings; 2-4 hectares is 11.8 per cent; 4-10 hectares is 5.5 per cent; and more than 10 hectares is 1.2 per cent of all holdings.

10 For details of the technological approach as solution to the problems see the Report by the National Farmers' Commission (2006); Govt. of Karnataka (2002), and the large number of official reports related to addressing agricultural distress.

11 The continued negligence of agricultural issues by the State, especially since the period of economic liberalisation has been highlighted by many scholars (see Patnaik 2004, Sharma 2006, Harriss-White 2004).

12 During 1998, when farmers' suicides were reported from different parts of the country, the "Forum of Farmers Organisations on Globalisation and Agriculture" held a workshop in New Delhi and passed resolutions demanding safeguards for small and marginal farmers from the onslaught of WTO. This was not followed by any active mobilisation of peasants at the field level. However, in Ananthapur district the All India Kisan Sabha (AIKS) associated with CPI (M) has organised protest marches and voiced concern about farmers' suicides in different forums. During the Asian Social Forum meet at Hyderabad held in January 2003, a public hearing on farmers' suicide was organised by the AIKS. The issue of farmers' suicides has been raised in the legislative assemblies of the respective states by the opposition parties. (Ref. R.M. Vidyasagar and Suman Chandra COUNTERCURRENTS.ORG (http://agrariancrisis.wordpress.com/farmers-suicides/farmers%E2%80%99-suicides-in-andhra-pradesh-and-karnataka-nird-study).

13 *The Times of India*, May 11th, 2010.

14 The National Commission for Farmers also submitted a new National Policy for Farmers in 2006 to the Government.

15 The CPI (M) report cards (2009) on UPA government's performance provide a trenchant criticism of the failures and limitations of these rural programmes.

16 Drawing on C.K. Prahlad's best selling book, *The Fortune at the Bottom of the Pyramid* (2004), several marketing agencies and business houses

are now recognizing the potential of the rural masses and their consumer capacities.

17 *The Times of India*, May 12, 2010.

18 Between the periods of 2004 to 2010, there have been three major reports assessing the poverty levels in the nation. Each of these has come out with different levels; in 2004, the Planning Commission considered 27.5 per cent of the population to be below poverty levels; the Saxena Committee revised it to be at least 50 per cent, and the Suresh Tendulkar committee (in 2010) considered it to be around 37.5 per cent. The World Bank considers 41.6 per cent of the population in India to be below poverty. These measurements and assessments are a political issue and the debates continue.

This bottle of pesticide will always be an option…

Agriculturist to the Perspectives Team, 2009

Agrarian riots may become the normal state of things throughout India. Let us not be too sure that these silent millions will remain in silence and patience forever. The dumb shall speak and the deaf shall hear.

Eduardo Galeano, *Mirrors: Stories of Almost Everyone*, 2009

Chapter Six

Involutions and the Significance of 'Agrarian Suicides'

> ...Food Corporation of India godowns continue to burst at the seams with excess food stocks. The common sense idea of distributing some of this food to the poor seems to frighten economic advisers. With another bumper harvest ahead, the stocks will continue growing unless more is distributed.
>
> **Jean Dreze, Economist, *The Hindustan Times*, October 14, 2010**

Several creative writers have captured and represented a range of conditions and experiences that mark the lives of different rural citizens. Mahasweta Devi's (1998) poignant and sharp narratives from the Adivasi/tribal regions illustrate a range of life conditions, struggles and violences. In *Bitter Soil* she describes how desperate Adivasis in the forests of Palamau take to consuming the seeds distributed by the government for food production. Starving, they compete with wild animals for resources such as a salt lick, and are themselves killed by an elephant, which in turn is declared a rogue by the forest department. In his novel *Uchalya* (The Branded) Laxman Gaikwad (1998) captures the lives of people once branded as 'criminal tribes' and details their struggle for social recognition and political assertion. The angst and contradictions of different caste groups as they are caught between officially declared policies and programmes formulated by the government and the subversion of these by caste and village hierarchies in Andhra Pradesh are described and detailed by Kalipatnam Rama Rao (2006). A bitter harvest awaits the protagonists of Lokesh Agasanakatte's (2007) story, '*The Rabi Harvest*', when Dalit cultivators, who have received land distributed by the government, work the land with enthusiasm and hard effort, pooling in their hard-earned savings to buy hybrid sunflower seeds, only to see that the seeds yield an abundance of stalks that have no sunflower seeds. And the promise and failure of elementary education is represented in Shantabai Kamble's (1992) narrative '*Naja Goes to School – and Doesn't*', when an intelligent and hardworking Mahar girl's education is disrupted as she cannot afford to enroll in a high school located away from her village. Capturing the tragi-comedy of village life, now under the dictates of a new market ethos, Poornachandra Tejaswi (2006) in his *Mayaloka (*World of Illusions*)* details how agriculturists take great risk and trouble to grow new commercial crops but the alliances between liquor contractors and government officials break their resolution to stage a non-violent agitation for fair crop prices.

In these and other descriptions from different regions of India one sees recurring conditions and experiences: the utter degradation of life despite the hard work; the denial of justice; the tyranny of customary and bureaucratic powers; the frustration of witnessing the declaration of a range of 'rights' that are not realised; and the growing aspirations for a better life and the multiple forms of violence within and between communities.

These narratives and their representations of rural life have had resonances for me and in many ways they encapsulate the complex trends in rural India. Travelling frequently between Bangalore and various rural areas all over India,[1] I have often been struck by the contradictory conditions that constitute life in rural India. Promising and positive initiatives that fail to take root, opportunities that go awry or to the most undeserving, the stoic stance of the most marginalised, and among the people an overall sense of forbearance despite the load of multiple indignities.

Aligning the narratives and details of the suicides by agriculturists with conditions such as those described above, enables us to assess and understand the contemporary predicament of rural India. For this predicament is not a condition that can be read through the singular 'Agrarian Question', that rests on an assumed teleology of an inevitable period of transition, but can be seen as reflecting and responding to the multiple 'Agrarian Questions'.[2] These questions can be linked to at least eight factors or conditions and relate to that of: class relations, forms of wage labour, political mobilisation, the creation of a pool of reserve labour, food security, gender relations, ecological conditions, and the question of knowledge forms. To locate and understand the predicament of contemporary rural India requires the highlighting of all these conditions and trends and the need to go beyond the debate on the untidiness associated with inevitable shifts from predominantly pre-capitalist to capitalist forms of agriculture and agrarian societies. For what we are witness to in much of rural India are complex conditions where even as elements from pre-capitalist agriculture are retained (as that of caste-based structure of agriculture and the vast pool of unfree labour), it is not merely capital that impacts the characteristics of agriculture (and its structure, pattern, productivity, labour etc.). While these are important, attention must also be paid to the interlinkages between the social structure of agriculture, and its linkages to the larger political and economic dynamics, and to the social world and its old and new pressures which coalesce to form configurations which in their complexity and implications stand as the predicament of rural India.

Conditions of 'Involutions' in Rural India

These complexities and their implications for the predicament of rural India can perhaps be framed and understood through what

Clifford Geertz defined as 'involution', a process of simultaneous retention of pre-existing and established structures and the adoption and integration of newer forms and practices which lead to internal complexities.[3] The retention of caste as the social bases/structure for agriculture, and therefore of the predominantly agrarian economies and social worlds of India in general and of rural economies in particular, and the interlinkages of such a retained structure with the forces of democracy, new economic trends, especially that of the neo-liberal agenda, and altering social aspirations form the bedrock for this involution. The introduction of new subjectivities and the imbalances between economic and political power, linked to the spread of electoral democratic demands, have created new forms of tension that erupt into forms of collective and public violence. The intrusion of capital and market into the interiority of both non-capitalist and pre-capitalist economies and societies and the subsequent rendering of rural citizens into subjects, who are targeted to be at the receiving end of new strategies of governmentality[4] and/or the market, mark the contemporary predicament of rural India. These involutions in rural India can be discerned at multiple levels and as the complexity of each articulates with the other, they consolidate the forms of inequities and violence in the life-worlds of rural residents and of the rural as a site and space.

Accumulation by Dispossession and Simultaneous Welfare Governmentality

Perhaps one of the sharpest forms of involution has resulted from the presence of both: the intensification of forms of 'accumulation by dispossession'[5] (see Sanyal 2008) along with a range of new strategies of governmentality. As new global capital enters even remote areas, it has rendered vast numbers of rural residents into conditions of displacement and disenfranchisement. Few trends exemplify this better than that of the entry and presence of national and international corporate groups into rural areas in search of minerals and natural resources. Growing expropriation of natural resources has been facilitated through policies such as the liberalisation of mining and the promotion of extractive industries in prime forest and conservation lands. National and international corporate groups, backed by the State, seek to displace indigenous people and rural and agrarian livelihoods by cordoning off vast tracts for mining minerals. The subsequent contestations over land, resources, and rights have rendered vast tracts of rural belts from those in the interiors of Chhattisgarh, Jharkhand, and Orissa, to the agricultural belts of Bellary in north Karnataka, and coastal belts in Goa and Maharashtra into contested terrains. These processes encapsulate questions and issues of land rights, environmental concerns and the erosion of democratic processes in the name of expediting economic growth. The deployment of 'Operation Green Hunt',[6] to cleanse 'naxal or extremist infested areas' which also targets not merely political dissidents but the working poor, especially the disenfranchised Adivasis or tribals, highlights for us the rendering of the rural into a battle ground. Similar conditions of disruption and violence have marked large swathes of the North-East where long-drawn contestations over Indian hegemony are buttressed by growing inter-ethnic group tensions and the new capitalist expansion into the region. Each encounter and the subsequent loss of life and the disruption of life in these regions reinforce the key contradiction in which the fundamental rights to life, livelihood, and democracy are being eroded and denied even as at the national level a new regime of rights – to food, education, information, forest etc. – are sought to be promoted and ensured.

The growing demands made on the rural hinterlands, as the metropolises expand and receive make-over to become 'world class cities', have left vast tracts eroded and a large number of agriculturists displaced. The visual violence on the landscape is only the symptom of the deeper violence that has ensued since the land grabbing. Village after village, in the vicinity of the metropolises or in zones identified for future industrial establishments, are submitting to the land mafia and many have traded their agricultural livelihoods and lives to become either a new class of the idle, supported by land sales, or the displaced. The commoditisation of land has extended to plantations and scenic spots which are now altered to cater to urban needs and desires, and are being shifted from being sites of long-term production and employment to becoming resorts: the occasionally but luxuriously used sites for a privileged elite. The negative impact of all of these, and the dispensation of agriculturists into low-grade and servile service economy, are yet to be fully recognised by policy makers.

In the unchecked land grabbing, large tracts of land lie marred and abused. Environmental and economic rights related to land, water, and energy use are bypassed for commercial interests of real estate development. Despite the hype of using Information Technology to regulate land market, transactions related to land continue to be mired in complex and dense rules. The violence of displacement by dams, declaring of forests as reserved areas, cordoning off large tracts of regions for mining and other resource extraction purposes have, in the past decade (2000-2010) reached unprecedented levels. Even as the few right-to-land movements (e.g. the *Janadesh* movement) and more recently the walk undertaken by *Kisan Swaraj Yatra*[7] have called for judicious and democratic rights to land, the government has facilitated the opening of the land market to national and global players. Envisaged as inevitable market rules that propel economic growth, new policies are being formulated that will facilitate the transfer of even fertile agricultural land into the hands of the land mafia. Resistances and criticisms have been stifled by a State that has adjusted itself to the demands of global capital and does not secure the rights and interests of disadvantaged citizens.

The strength of the peoples' movements in Singur and Nandigram, in which forced industrialisation was questioned (Datta 2008) and the land-grab thwarted, and the contestations over mining licenses in Niyamagiri in Orissa[8] are emblematic of peoples' resistance to forced and undemocratic land acquisition. But, these may also be the only exceptions to the otherwise quiet but steady submissions and transformations that are taking place in the name of land acquisition.

In the passage of the nation to a global, real estate grid, land has become a signal commodity and symbol through which the processes of exploitation, violation of rights take place and the very foundations of a democratic polity and society are being eroded. A primarily neo-liberal model that permits the complete marketisation of land is exacerbating the long-standing and vexatious problems not only of land denial to a majority of citizens but is also the foundation on which a range of tensions between agricultural vs. industrial use of land, rural vs. urban growth, and market demand vs. ecological sustainability are being played out. New land policies are part of the new governance preferences and seek to uphold "land over inhabitants" (Datta 2008: 32). But land itself is primarily being constituted, transacted and related to as a commodity, as real estate units whose ownership is determined by the highest bidder. And the State itself has in all these cases become the facilitator of the conversion of vast tracts of land into corporate property and acts at the behest of corporate groups.

But even as these processes and forces of appropriation are deployed in the name of expediting economic growth and alleviating poverty, the government's range of programmes form a part of 'welfarist governmentality' (Sanyal 2008:221). The myriad range of programmes (see Chapter Five) in various states indicates how such 'governmentality' seeks to alleviate the very depredations of the intrusion of capital. The resulting contradictions in the economy and in the conditions of the working poor are captured by Sanyal who notes how "...in the simultaneous presence of these two processes, their mutuality and contradictions, (is) what constitutes the dynamics of post-colonial capitalism in the era of globalisation; forces of globalisation are simultaneously enabling and constraining, empowering, and debilitating" (2008:220). Much of this is relevant and visible in the agrarian context, where the new regime of commercial agriculture is constructed and engaged with as a way out of disadvantage but is also the source of distress. The palliative politics deployed by the government then acts as the band-aid that prevents further mobilisation against the system or the search for alternatives. In addition, the very involutions in the power bases of rural India compound this disarray.

Contestations over Power

The potential and strengths of democracy and its articulations with the specificities of regional caste structures have also led to involutions in the power structures and relations in rural areas. Caste-based reservations in political structures and processes have resulted in an imbalance in the power relations between caste groups. Entrenched and actual economic power continues to vest with upper and dominant castes, but political power is being gradually claimed by low-ranked caste groups. The resulting imbalance which is manifested in multiple contestations has also become the source of reinforced forms of violence against the lower castes. Tarauli in Uttar Pradesh, Kamballapalli in Karnataka, Khairlanji in Maharashtra, Kodiyamkulam in Tamil Nadu, where Dalits families have been subject to mass killing, torching of homes and destruction of property by local upper castes or by rival caste groups, are now testimonies to the recurring caste-based violence in rural India.

In addition to such tensions and violence, democratic decentralisation as reposed and instituted in the revised versions of decentralised governance as the Panchayat Raj structures in the rural areas has also invoked novel forms of resistance by dominant and upper caste groups. Refusing to submit to norms of democracy in which low-ranked caste members may occupy positions of decision-making, upper castes such as the Rajputs and Jats in the Haryana and Punjab belts have resorted to invoking and re-constituting caste panchayats as a way to defy democratic norms and regulations. The spread of Khap Panchayats in the Haryana belt and Khatta Panchayats in Tamil Nadu are representative of such trends.

Internal Violence and Creation of the Dispensable

A third feature of the involution can be observed in the extent to which economic development has not in many cases translated into social development for all. Few cases represent this better than that of the spread of forms of anti-girl child sentiments and actions which have led to the continously declining sex ratio in the country. As studies have documented,[9] the culling of female foetuses and the resorting to female infanticide have become rampant not so much in the areas that are economically disadvantaged or among disadvantaged social and caste groups but in regions such as Haryana and Punjab, among the economically better off, and in pockets such as in Salem and Dindigul districts of Tamil Nadu, which have recorded economic prosperity, and among dominant caste groups (Harriss-White 1999). Cultural orientations such as son preference and male inheritance of property, especially land, have combined with the new pressures of dowry practices, compulsions of smaller family size, decreasing land resources and increasing costs of upbringing to lead to an intensification of discrimination against girl children. New medical technologies and sex selective abortions have aided such culling (and have resulted in the decline in sex ratio, now sharply visible in the age-group of below six years (2001 census 927 girls to 1000 boys) and have tremendous significance for future gender relations. The results of sharp sex ratio declines are already being experienced in the very belts that had intensified gender culling. As Ravinder Kaur (2008) reports for the Punjab, brides are not only being imported from regions across the nation (with implications for their status and well-being) but the phenomena of large numbers of bachelors has also become an additional problem in several villages. But going beyond the thesis of a cultural bias against girls, Kaur points to the spread of the desire to have single sons which is linked to the "...precariousness of agricultural livelihoods that explains the desire for a family consisting of a single son. As the benchmark for living standards continues to rise and with it the costs of living, and agricultural yields plateau, the desire is to put all one's eggs in the basket of a single son." (Kaur 2008: 114). The family, for long a site of contestations and of deep gender discrimination, is now placed on the national terrain as a site where the interlinkages between uneven economic development and iniquitous social structures hold sway.

If the above involutions operate at the level of the economic, political, and social spheres and indicate the resulting conditions of distress and violence that they produce in the lives of rural citizens, then the involutions produced at the deeper level of culture have significance for the identities and sociality of all rural residents.

From Agricultural Pluralism to Political Culturalism

If pluralism itself is to be understood as more than the heterogeneity of visible cultures and practices, there is the need to see pluralism as a way of life, limited not only to a specific geo-political territory and to its inhabitants but as also linked to symbols, memories, and identities (Nagaraj 1998). To this one can add the centrality of knowledge forms, which made agriculture a way of life and which contained within its heterogeneity a framework that generated and sustained a lived pluralism. India's agriculture had long been associated with a diversity that resulted from a combination of a wide variety of agro-ecological zones[10] and a plurality of cultures. Ludden notes that historically,

"Each agricultural zone had its own style of life, for farming routines and material conditions dominated human experience" (1985:61). A result of this was sharply varied and identifiable regional agri-cultural complexes in which each region had its own cultivation patterns, knowledge systems associated with them, and socio-economic relations and political structures. Even differences in language were subsumed by the specificities of agri-cultural complexes to lend regions their specific identities and orientation. An example of this is the dry, semi-arid zone of the western Deccan belt which has a similar and shared agri-cultural complex despite the geo-physiographic region being divided between the states and linguistic zones of Maharashtra and Karnataka and of the language differences of Marathi and Kannada respectively. Associated with each agri-cultural complex were also the region-specific rituals, customs, linkages, relationships and status norms that different groups had (Robb 1996). Invoking or highlighting the cultural importance of pluralistic agriculture and the role of agriculturists bears the burden of being possible representations of the rural and the agrarian as new myths, the romanticisation of lives without attention to their class position and implications (Brass 2000). Yet there is need to recognise the links between regionally specific knowledge forms and cultures as the erosion of this form of lived and enabling pluralism has implications for the growth of singular and dominant forms of culturalism which is a result of the fragmentation of the collective, locally embedded practices of agriculture. The erosion of localised, heterogenous forms of agri-cultures, the promotion of technology, capital, and external knowledge-based agricultural models for commercial purposes, and the failure to address the social bases of the agrarian structure – all compound the conditions of involutions in rural India. The promotion of corporate agri-business interests (with the emphasis on biotechnology, genetically modified organisms, and a range of new inputs and high capital and new intellectual property regimes) have implications for the very foundational premises of India's pluralism.

In the context of increasingly widespread rural tensions, the double loss of both – a livelihood and an enabling culture – has compelled many to go into 'cultural mourning' (Kakkar 1997; passim), a situation in which groups bemoan real and imaginary cultural losses as the bases of their problems and submit themselves to forms of cultural mobilisation and religious fundamentalism. This has been observed in the results of the Green Revolution in Punjab. When land and its associated culture were no longer the central symbols, a fundamentalist version of Sikhism filled the gap (Shiva 1991). In Karnataka, agendas and policies that have unleashed intense forms of capital intrusion have also fostered a sense of displacement among many local groups and networks. Even as a booming international economy, and its associated life-style has gained mainstay, several organisations which have support from rural and semi-rural residents, such as the Karnataka Rakshana Vedike (Protect Karnataka Forum), Kannada Sene (Kannada Army) and Jai Karnataka (Hail Karnataka) that claim to champion the interests of the region and state in linguistic and exclusionary terms have gained space and members in the public canvas of the region. The growth of caste-based federations and political mobilisation across the nation also testify to this. The mobilisation of Uttar Pradesh's Yadavs under the umbrella of being 'Krishnavanshi' or 'descendents of Krishna' (Michelutti 2008), the coming together of Jats in the Haryana belt, and the organisation of Bumihars in Bihar represent such cases.

As organisations and associations that draw on cultural and religious symbols grow, and gain legitimacy and presence as sources to alleviate the growing cultural and social alienation and forms of economic oppression, they deploy exclusionary symbols and agendas that threaten the very constitutive pluralism of the nation. Gujarat's disembedded agrarian social formation that has been witness to the sharp polarisation of caste, tribal, and religious groups (Breman 2003, Gidwani 2008) and which culminated into the genocide of Muslims in 2002, and the subsequent deep fracturing of the regional cultural corpus, is one other case of such loss of pluralism in the face of intrusive capital and external knowledge forms. In Orissa, the spread and intensification of violence against Adivasis and Christians can be linked to the growing dislocation and fragmentation of groups that once had worked together in local forms of agriculture (Chatterji 2009).

Although Gandhi largely overlooked the political and economic dimensions of rural communities, and most specifically their role in reproducing the hierarchical and iniquitous caste system, he recognised the importance of decentralised, plural, rural cultures. Asserting the importance of agriculture as a vocation, he believed it to be capable of being the seedbed of *Swaraj*: the new ethically and morally grounded form of 'self-rule' that would enable India to not only break away from colonialism but also generate a new civilisation.[11] Yet, post colonial agricultural policies have moved far from this emphasis on establishing viable rural communities. Agriculture and agrarian cultures are increasingly integrated into a global regime that privileges elite consumption and the transformation of land and agriculture into commodities over ecological and social sustainability. Despite volumes of studies and evidence that the Green Revolution model of agriculture is not ecologically, economically and socially tenable, there are no serious official or government driven attempts to seek localised and multiple alternatives. Instead there seems to be an intensification of the external, technology and science driven models in which new inputs such as Bt cotton and other genetically modified organisms and seeds are sought to be promoted, and are ways in which the presence of corporate groups in the agricultural sector is being facilitated. Recent state government attempts to recognise and promote organic agriculture, without paying attention to the structure of agriculture and its iniquitous foundation, are also problematic in as much as they seek to mark and reclaim agriculture as another domain of a 'pure' India, one more domain to be reclaimed as part of a past heritage[12] (which are themselves constructs).

If the plural agro-ecologies, located within hierarchical structures, were worked on by the imprint of the cultural collective on agriculture, then individuated agricultural regimes privilege productivity but also generate forms of ecological, economic and social unsustainability. The combined deficits of both – an iniquitous structure of the old and the burdens of an external model of the contemporary – envelop a significant proportion of the agricultural population, with the marginal and low-ranked caste groups and women bearing the most severe burdens. These conditions and trends have become the foundations on which the very life of agriculturists has become precarious and many consider it to be not worth either being in agriculture or to be alive itself.

Social Position and Symbolic Representation of Agriculturists

At independence and in the following two decades (1950s to 1960s), the agriculturist as '*kisan*' (farmer, cultivator, peasant) was the foremost iconic figure of a free India. Characteristics typically associated with the '*kisan*' were that of the hard-working cultivator, the long-suffering subject of colonialism whose time to be released from rent-racking and forms of servitude had come, the model citizen whose primary duties of provisioning for the nation (as *annadata*, the giver of rice/food) kept the nation indebted to him. But over the years, and sharply evident since the late 1990s, the figure of the *Kisan* has receded from public memory and associations with positive aspects of nation-building. Even as the rhetoric of the new global, high-technology led economy and of the possibilities of a 'new India' have taken centre-stage, the image and representation of the *Kisan* have altered significantly. Now the agriculturist is seen as a category of economic worker, an agent in the livelihood called agriculture, and as a resident of a 'village', a voter in the village constituency and is rendered into three related but different positions: as redundant, as a supplicant, and as a patient.

Shifts to an urban, service economy are seen and represented as inevitable and the large mass of agriculturists are seen as redundant to the new work force and economy. While actual economic policies place the burden of entrepreneurship and independent abilities on each agriculturist, regional and central level programmes, waiver of loans, and special 'packages' reduce them to becoming supplicants who expect a range of welfare measures and support systems.

In seeking to ameliorate agricultural distress or in providing allocations of funds and support, the agriculturist is increasingly constructed and represented in policy circles and programmes as a patient who needs to be rescued and sustained. As with the policies that overlook the structural features of agriculture and rural society, and those that try to fit agriculturists into the larger capitalist system, such demands overlook the heterogeneity of agricultural forms in the nation, its foundation as the bases of its pluralism, and of the inability of the new globalizing economy to integrate them as key players in the nation's economic games.

Disenchantment with Agriculture

Dislodged from any position of significance in the national imaginary, unassisted in the struggle for decent livelihoods and social mobility, a majority of agriculturists now consider agriculture to be a losing game. Among many there is now widespread disenchantment with agriculture as a livelihood and as a way of life. What is emerging in several pockets of the nation are trends of not only increasing diversification of occupations and the shift towards non-agricultural rural livelihoods (Gupta 2004; Sainath 2009) but also the seeking to be out of agriculture. Once cited as a way of life and as the foundation of Indian civilisation itself, many agriculturists now no longer see agriculture as a vocation to be proudly associated with. As some of my old friends from a village in Bijapur narrated to me, "to be in agriculture now is to be ruined" and they do not expect their children or progeny to be called agriculturists (*Raitha*), once considered to be the 'food giver' and therefore the 'life giver' itself to the rest of the nation.

The need to be out of agricultural and caste-based occupations is linked to both the largely un-remunerative bases of agriculture and the sense of deep futility and frustration it seems to bring. One reason why even blatant and rapacious rural land grab projects have not been challenged uniformly across the nation emanates from the construction of the rural and agricultural as burdensome which many seek to move away from (Vijaybhaskar 2010). Discontent against the world of agriculture is now being expressed through rumblings against the deep frustrations and futility with the life-world of rurality; in the sacrifices made to send sons to urban areas that fail to garner them jobs; in the sale of land to pay for the dowries of daughters; in the endless chasing of paper; abandoning homes to seek employment elsewhere; in their witness to the growing forms of corruption and venality; in tightening their belts on already hard-pressed stomachs; in return trips to the village that they must make to sustain their families; and in the ways in which they salvage their sense of self and moor their collective identities.

In the introduction to his classic book, *Pig Earth*, John Berger provides a sharp critique of the destruction of the peasantries of the world and highlights how: "His [the peasant's] conditions of living, the degree of his exploitation and his suffering may be desperate, but he cannot contemplate the disappearance of what gives meaning to everything he knows, which is, precisely, his will to survive" (1979/1992: xx). The predicament of most of India's agriculturists seems to be precisely this, the 'disappearance of what gives meaning to everything' they know. From its bases in the ecological specificity of each region and the shared pattern, knowledge and process of agriculture to the current emphasis on engaging with an externally formulated model which has led to the loss of the cultural basis of agriculture, the knowledge dissonance, and to the individualisation of agriculturists, the current predicament is one of intense distress which is represented in the conditions of loss of meaning, confusion and disorientation among cultivators. That most victims choose to end their lives by consuming pesticides symbolises the key source of distress; agriculture itself and its new inputs, engaging with which has led to their ruination. As one of the women from a family which had lost its sole earning member to suicide said to me, "agriculture is a noose around our necks".

Significance of the Suicides

In having consigned the suicides by agriculturists to a 'shadow space', government, media, and the larger society have failed to assess the implications of such deaths for the very fabric of the larger society and the nation at large. The suicides by agriculturists in India are emblematic of the deep structural deficits and problems of rural India and the agrarian economy and polity. The intrusion of the market under such conditions has also meant significant shifts in the life-worlds of agriculturists. These have combined, since 1997, with the beginning of the spate of suicides, to render rural India into conditions of economic retrogression, political marginalisation, and social involution. Linked to these trends, the suicides must be seen as situationally fostered acts which are located on the economic and social template of the life of marginalised agriculturists. From their attempts to rise out of conditions of deprivation and disadvantage, and in their search and assertion for recognition and resemblance, marginal agriculturists take on the additional burden of multiple risks. Without adequate scaffolding by the State or local society, they face production loss or economic decline with social and moral scarring. They confront and experience intense social and individual degradation at multiple levels: attempting to overcome generational, collective and individual disadvantages; tolerating multiple forms of humiliation; and experiencing the loss of crops and the inability to sustain families. Each of these compounds the deep erosion that they experience as individuals and as agriculturists whose livelihood and life is rendered as redundant and which erases all their efforts and their sense of self. Each loss (of crop, of economic viability and independence) and each failure (to rise out of conditions of disadvantage) reconstitutes them into the very structures of power and indignities that they sought to escape from.

In the larger consigning of the agrarian suicides to a 'shadow space' by the State, the dominant society, and the media, the deaths of the agriculturists have, over the years, been understood and represented as caused primarily by economic factors. What have been overlooked are the details of the conditions and trends which frame and mark the lives of the marginal majority. Unpacking the reasons and factors that led to the epidemics of suicide is to point not only to just the underbelly of a new but accelerated globalising economy but to also review these deaths as manifestations of the complexities and problems of retained hierarchical structures that intermingle with the new logics of expanding markets, intrusive capital, altered subjectivities, and varied knowledge forms. If the famines of the late nineteenth and twentieth century acted as 'engines of historical transformation' making once self-reliant and pre-modern societies into impoverished societies and marking them as 'Third World' nations, (Davis 2001: 15), then what significance do these suicides bode for Indian society and the nation?

Historically, agrarian crises have played a major role in the unmaking and remaking of several nations. The disembedding of agriculture in Europe led to the settling of the Americas, the Irish potato famine triggered an exodus that led to the formation of a world-wide Irish diaspora, Germany's agricultural crisis formed the bedrock of the genesis of the Nazi regime, forced agricultural collectivisation in the former Soviet Union and China led to famines and mass deaths. More recently, the sporadic uprisings of peasants in the Latin Americas such as that in Chiapas (Mexico), sought to defy the neglect and violence of rightist regimes. In Brazil, the failure of several governments over centuries to allocate land and resources has led to intense forms of violence against the working class, peasants and labour unions. In West Africa's Niger delta, the disruption of the riverine agrarian economy by the 'black gold' or oil industry has resulted prolonged regional and national level violence and conflict.

Gathering force at the turn of the twenty-first century, these agrarian suicides encapsulate the range of problems that mark agriculture the world over. While high productivity and an attendant loss of biodiversity have become markers of all new agricultural practices, most agriculturists are now faced with mounting debts and many are unable to make a living out of it. Indebtedness, loss of production, unviable livelihoods, food insecurity, and continuous loss of their capabilities to sustain themselves mark the lives of most cultivators. The result is that of a sharp erosion of agriculturists everywhere (Akram-Lodhi and Kay 2009) and their location into the structures of informal economies[13] (Sanyal 2008) and into conditions of distress. The suicides by agriculturists in India are also a part of the larger story and experiences of disembedding economies and societies which meet with economic and technological regimes that erode existing knowledge systems and where new economic cultures induce new aspirations. The flow of capital and the range of new goods, life-styles and aspirations have created social tremors among people who are newly integrated into the circuits of capital production and consumption. The resulting 'ethos of gambling' (Comaroff and

Comaroff 2001) that is now pervasive among new capitalists becomes both the source of possible escape from disadvantage and the source of risk and self destruction. Julie Livingston's study of widespread suicides in Botswana, Africa, highlights this and has resonance in the factors that compel India's agriculturists to commit suicide. "Suicides tell us much about loneliness, yet this loneliness is more complicated than popular Durkheimian invocations of anomie would have us believe. It is not that social life has atrophied or constricted so much as the relations between self and others have shifted in disorienting ways as consumption and sociality stoke one another. Novel investment opportunities are often carried out alone, as secrets. Yet they hinge on the dense interrelationships between material wealth (consumer goods) and social connections, and the shame of failed investment is often public" (2009: 675).

Over the years, the nature of suicides by agriculturists has also changed. Starting with individuals, primarily men in the prime ages of 28-45 years, dying in their homes or on their agricultural land, suicides now include deaths of whole families. In some cases, agriculturists have resorted to threats and attempts to commit collective or group suicide in order to press their demands.[14] Suicide notes by victims indicate not merely a self-blame but an attempt to highlight the factors and forces that have enforced many to resort to this desperate act. That the voice of agriculturists in distress points to these conditions of utter degradation and to the despondency that marks their lives is exemplified in the poignant and sharp letter addressed by an agriculturist[15], who then committed suicide.

On April 7th, 2010, in Maharashtra's Dhotragaon village in Washim district, Shri. Ramachandra Raut, an agriculturist, purchased a legal bond paper for rupees one hundred, and on it he addressed a letter to the Chief Minister, the Deputy Chief Minister, the Prime Minister, and to 'Madam Pratibhatai (Mother Pratibha)' Patil, the President of India. (See pages 189-191).

Raut's suicide note
(Written in Marathi; for translation see p. 189)

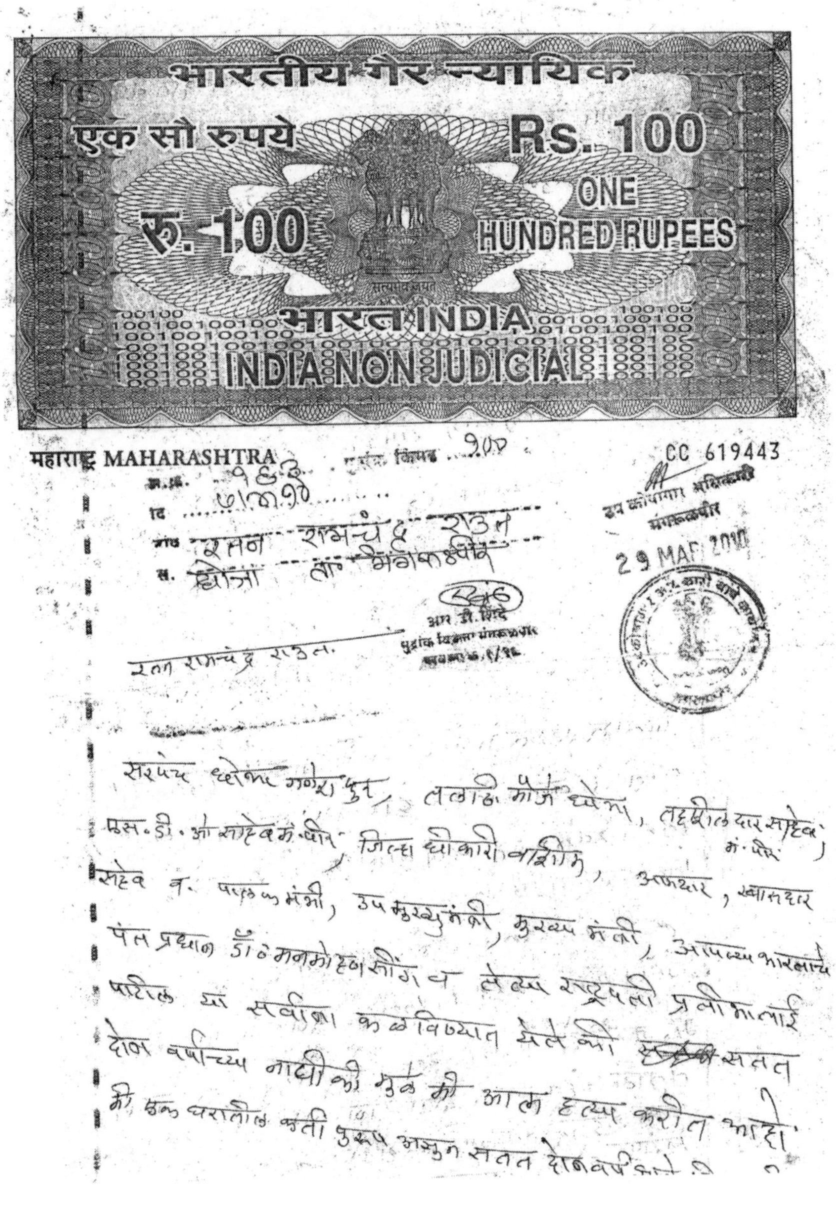

पानी नाही म्हणुन माझ्यावर हा टाईम आला आहे.
हे पुर्ण लेखी लिहुन देतो की सलग दोन वर्षाच्या नापीकी मुळे मी हे काम केले आहे माझ्यावर स्टेट बँकेचे कर्ज आहे व माझी सुन कोमी हिच्यावर सुध्दा स्टेट बँकेचे कर्ज आहे. आणि मुलगा गजानन याचेवर को ऑपरेटीव बँकेचे कर्ज आहे ते बँक वाले कर्जाच्यासाठी घरी येणार आले तर सतत दो वर्षाच्या नापीकी मुळे कर्ज कसे फेडावे असा विचार करुन मी माझे जीवन यात्रा संपवीली. तरी वरील सर्व वरीष्ठ अधीकाऱ्यानी याची नोंद घ्यावी हि विनंती.

आपला विश्वासु रतनराव आर राऊत.

X — X — X

पोलीस स्टेशन मंगरुळपीर

पोलीस स्टेशन मं.पीर यांनी माझ्या घरातील एकाही व्यक्तीचे बयान लिहुन घेउ नये. कारण हे बयान मी स्वत: लिहुन ठेवले आहे. कर्ज बाजारी मुळे व सतत दोन वर्षाच्या नापीकी मुळे माझ्यावर हा टाईम आला.

तलाठी मौजे धोत्रा यांनी वरील चौकशी करुन याची नोंद करा आणि माझा व सुनेचे, मुलाचे पुर्ण कर्ज माफ करुन मे. जुन महिने पुढील २००० चे पीक कर्ज देण्यात यावे यांना तलाठी साहेब यांनी ध्यान घेणे नाही तर या उभयतावर असा टाईम आला नाही पाहीजे. बरे असो मी आता कायमचा निरोप घेतो. रतनराव आर राऊत.

Translation

MAHARASHTRA
Date: 7/04/10
Place: Dhotra; Taluk (Mandal): Mangarulpir
Ratan Ramachandra Raut

To: Ganesh Druv, Sarpanch; the talathi (accountant) village Dhotra; Tehsildar, Mangarulpir; S.D.O, Mangrulpir; District Collector, Washim; Shri MLA and MP; Shri Palak Mantri (minister in charge of the district); the Deputy Chief Minister; the Chief Minister; Dr. Manmohan Singh, the Prime Minister of India, and Pratibhatai Patil, Madam President –

(It is) conveyed that the lack of harvest for two years in succession has led me to commit suicide.

I am the earning member of the family. Two years in succession, (there is) no yield, no water – which has brought me these (hard) times. I give this in writing that I have done this because of the lack of yield for two consecutive years. I took a loan from the State Bank. So did my eldest daughter-in-law. My son Gajanan has a loan from the Cooperative Bank. The Bank officials came home twice, and thinking about how to pay back the loans, given that we have had no yield for two-years long – I have decided to end my life. It is my request that the aforementioned officers take note of this.

* * *

For Police Station, Mangarulpir

The Police Station at Mangarulpir should not register a statement from a single member in my family. Because, I, myself, have written this statement. Indebtedness and consecutive two-years of no yield have brought me these times.

* * *

The *talathi* (village accountant) at Dhotra please inquire and record this. And the loan in its entirety incurred by me, my daughter-in-law and son may be forgiven. And they be given loans in May/June for the year 2010. Mr. *talathi*, please make a note of this. Both of them should not have (to face) the same fate. Alright. I will take your leave forever.

Ratanrao R. Raut.

In legalizing or seeking to make legal and formal his complaints and in listing the problems of agriculturists, Shri Raut, perhaps, sought to do through his suicide what he could not do in real life; that is, seek protection for his family and some solutions to the loaded problems of engaging in agriculture.

The shifting nature of the suicides – from individual acts conducted largely within the anonymity of their families to current trends where suicide notes address the government and/or political leaders and beseech support and remunerative prices – are representative of the new twist to the trend: the deployment of suicides as the last act of the desperate to speak in a political voice. In gaining 'epidemic' proportions the suicides have become both private and public acts that seek to call attention to the intense distress experienced by agriculturists. In their spread, intensity, and persistence over the past years (1997 onwards), the agrarian suicides are windows to understanding the trends and conditions in rural and agrarian India and of its twenty-first century predicament. In the details of the lives of the victims and of their compatriots are contained the narratives of the entry and consolidation of capital forces into the life-world of agriculturalists, the impact on retained and consolidated caste-based structures of accumulation, the erosion of local knowledge systems, the diffusion of new ideas and practices that are yet to gain mainstay, and the articulation between customary subjectivities and those that emanate from the new consumer cultures. In the inability to stem the suicides and/or to make those necessary structural alterations lies the failure of successive governments and the larger public. In sum the suicides encapsulate and represent a historical moment in the life of the nation. As the profits of a globalizing economy gain currency among the powerful, what we have is not a complete substitution of non/pre-capitalist structures and life-worlds for the new but an articulation of both in which the most vulnerable, the economically and socially marginal, have become victims. The suicides must be located at different levels: on the social and personal template of individual agriculturists who as risk-bearers and entrepreneurs seek a way out of a life of deprivation and disadvantage but become sacrificial victims to the very models that they seek to embrace; the opening and intrusion of the market and excessively commercialised media; and the spread of forms of modernity and social aspirations to until now relatively closed societies which makes possible opportunities and also expectations and stresses, especially for those who seek to engage with economic models that portend a new and better life.

The context of emergent socialities and cultures of rurality in which dual and contradictory pressures of being individualised economic actors but also collective cultural actors provides the social bases for inducing agriculturists into an economy of risk and vulnerability. And at the larger macro economic and political level in which State and market promote a model of economic development but provide no safety net to address failures, the risks undertaken by individual agriculturists become unbearable burdens. In taking their own lives, agriculturists seek to disengage from these burdens that erode their very sense of being.

If such trends continue, unaddressed and seen as part of the inevitable grand transformation that India must make to becoming a post-agricultural nation, then perhaps what Eric Hobsbawm (1994) noted as the most significant change of the twentieth century, that of the 'passing of the peasants', will in India be played out fully in the twenty-first century with the beginning of the death of its myriad forms of agricultures. Embedded in an unsustainable model of production, in which the significant symbols and meanings of agriculture and land itself are fast altering, and in which the State remains a duplicitous actor, the mass of rural subjects, marginalised and overlooked, will probably provide the labour on which the nation will march towards its urban shift and for which agriculturists will be largely unremunerated and unremembered.

But the current conditions of degradation and erosion in rural and agricultural economies and the rise of the urban as the key site of all future civilisations should not be the justifying or legitimizing narrative to see the end of local forms (and not necessarily peasant forms) of agriculture. New trends in Europe (Van der Ploeg 2010) and the United States (Berry 2004) and elsewhere indicate the urgent need to sustain multiple forms of agriculture and of retaining the rural bases of civilisation. Even as global urbanisation gains momentum, the possibility and need for "re-ruralising the world (so as) to recuperate the spirit as well as life" (Dalla Costa 2007: 118) of a majority of humans are issues that need serious attention. The failure to address the epidemics of suicides must now be compensated by addressing the long-entrenched structures and conditions which have rendered agriculturists vulnerable. This may be the way to remember these victims and the basis on which to reconstitute a more just and sustainable rurality in India.

Notes

1 In addition to eighteen months of ethnographic work in a village in Bijapur, Karnataka (1989-1990) and frequent visits and stays in Chamarajanagar district, Karnataka (from 2002 onwards), I have travelled to villages and rural sites all over India, including villages in Tamil Nadu, Andhra Pradesh, Kerala, Maharashtra, Gujarat, Madhya Pradesh, Rajasthan, Karnataka, Uttar Pradesh, Uttaranchal, Orissa, and Sikkim. During this period, I have visited and talked to people in about seventy eight villages and have details for forty six villages.

2 For an excellent summary of the 'Agrarian Question', from its mid nineteenth century source to that of the mid twentieth century and bringing it to the contemporary debates, see the essays by Akram-Lodhi and Kay (2010). Akram-Lodhi and Kay (2010) also elaborate on the

seven new agrarian questions that are pertinent to the global agrarian condition. To this I have added another, that of the question of knowledge forms as it is central to defining agricultural practices and hence linkages to the market.

3 Clifford Geertz first used the term 'agricultural involution' in his 1963 work on Indonesia. Drawing on Goldenweiser's descriptions of internally complex cultural patterns, Geertz used the term to refer to the forms by which Indonesia's colonial and post-colonial agriculture had retained its older forms and structures and yet absorbed the new, export cultivation of crops. Involution, according to him is "the overdriving of an established form in such a way that it becomes rigid through over elaboration of detail" (1963: 63). A large body of criticisms has been deployed against Geertz's description of Indonesia's agricultural economy, the most trenchant of which has been by Benjamin White (1983). A detailed response to these can be found in Geertz (2005). Burawoy's adaptation of the term 'involution' to understand post-Soviet Russian economy and society emphasises such complexity and adds to it the criteria of "degeneration of production, society and state to the expansion of the sphere of (market) exchange" (2002: 308). I have combined these two definitions to describe Indian rurality as being in a state of 'involution', marked by not only a retention of established structures, and integration of new patterns of production, but also by complexities and contradictions in the interlinks between economy, polity and society.

4 See Kalyan Sanyal (2008) for an excellent overview and analyses of the links between capital and labour, pre-capitalist and capitalist economies (including the informal and formal sectors) and the subsequent forms of governmentality that seek to link the two.

5 From Kalyan Sanyal's (2008) reference to David Harvey's reformulation of 'primitive accumulation' as that of 'accumulation by dispossession'.

6 Operation Green Hunt is the deployment of paramilitary forces by the Government of India to the central India belts of Chhattisgarh, Jharkhand, and Madhya Pradesh. The stated objectives are to prevent the spread of Maoist mobilisation in the areas but it is also one of the ways to facilitate capitalists', both national and international, access to the regions' natural resources.

7 The Kisan Swaraj Yatra was organised by the Alliance for Sustainable and

Holistic Agriculture (ASHA) and was initiated on October 2nd and after a walk through twenty states and culminated at New Delhi on December 11, 2010.

8 There are now environmental and human rights movements against the entry and exploitation of natural resources in tribal areas. One successful campaign, supported by international networks and activist groups, was the rejection of the attempts by the international mining companies Vedanta (U.K based) and Posco (Taiwan based) to extract mining leases in Orissa.

9 For an insightful overview of the issue of female foeticide and culling see the essay by Barbara Harriss-White (1999). Subsequent research that has documented this across the country are the studies by Mary John et al. (2009) and the work by Ravinder Kaur (2008).

10 Various scholars and projects have identified or classified rural India into different types of agro-ecological zones. The Peoples of India project had identified ninety-one types (see Singh 2001) and government-related schemes and programmes typically indicate India to have twenty types of agro-ecological regions and sixty agro-ecological sub-regions.

11 See Pinto (1998) for an elaboration on Gandhi's views on agriculture.

12 Some state government led programmes for the promotion of organic agriculture are not derived from assessments of the negative impact of the Green Revolution package but are instead drawn on ideas of reviving cultural heritage and practices. For example, the BJP government in Karnataka has promoted *savayava krishi* or 'organic agriculture' which draws on ideas of an ideal past and of Indian knowledge practices as superior. Further, the organic agriculture mission supported by the BJP government also draws on its network of affiliates to the RSS and other organisations.

13 Kalyan Sanyal (2008) reconceptualises and identifies 'the informal economy' as a 'need economy' (marked by inadequate access to capital) but not as a contradiction to the larger capital economy, but as complementary to it. While the term and its usage seem relevant to this study, I have not drawn on this for this book.

14 In Mysore, agriculturists who were demanding a hike in sugarcane prices, threatened to commit suicide in the Deputy Commissioner's office (*Vijaya Times*, 18th August, 2006). Similar threats and public

statements were issued when agriculturists were displaced for a large housing site in Bangalore. Other threats of mass or collective suicide have been recorded in the states of Maharashtra, West Bengal, and Orissa. The most recent one was on Feb 4th in Gulbarga district, Karnataka where twelve agriculturists attempted to commit suicide in the Tehsildar's office, citing their frustration and anger at low prices for red gram.

15 I thank P. Sainath for sending me a copy of the letter written by Shri Raut, and Shivali Tukdeo for translating the letter from Marathi to English.

References

Agarwal, Bina. 1997. 'Bargaining and Gender Relations: Within and Beyond the Household', *Feminist Economics*, 3(1).

Aggarwal, Rimjhim. 2006 'Resource Poor Farmers in South India: On the Margins or Frontiers of Globalisation?', Research Paper no. 2006/97. Tokyo: WIDER, United Nations University.

Agasanakatte, Lokesh. 2007. Mungarina Pairu (First Harvest). in *Hattiyemba Bhoomiya Tunuku*. Bangalore: Chanda Pustaka.

Akram-Lodhi, A. Haroon and Christobal Kay. 2009. *Peasants and Globalisation: Political Economy, Rural Transformation and the Agrarian Question*. London: Routledge.

Akram-Lodhi, A. Haroon. 2010. 'Modernising Subordination? A South Asian Perspective on the World Development Report 2008: Agriculture for Development', *Journal of Peasant Studies*, 36 (3).

Arvind. 2006. 'In India's Richest State, Suicides and Starvation Stalk the Countryside', *People's March*, 7(5).

Amin, Shahid. 1982. 'Small Peasant Commodity Production and Rural Indebtedness: the Culture of Sugarcane in Eastern U.P., c. 1880-1920', in *Subaltern Studies I: Writings on South Asian History and Society*, ed. Ranajit Guha. Delhi: Oxford University Press.

Balakrishnan, Pulapre et al. 2008. *Agricultural Growth in India since 1991*. Department of Economic Analysis and Policy. Mumbai: Reserve Bank of India.

Bauman, Zygmunt. 2001. *The Bauman Reader*, ed. Peter Beilharz. London: Blackwell Publishers.

——. 2004. *Wasted Lives: Modernity and its Outcasts*. Cambridge: Polity Press.

Bardhan, Pranab.1984. *The Political Economy of Development in India* (expanded new edition). New Delhi: Oxford University Press.

Batterbury, S.P.J. 1996. 'Planners or Performers? Reflections on Indigenous Dryland Farming in Northern Burkina Faso', *Agriculture and Human Values*, 13 (3).

Beck, Ulrich. 1999. *World Risk Society*. Cambridge: Polity Press.

Beck, Ulrich and Elizabeth Beck-Gernsheim. 2001. *Individualization: Institutionalized Individualism and its Social and Political Consequences*. London:Sage.

Berger, John. 1979/1992. *Pig Earth*. New York: Vintage International.

Berking, Helmuth. 1996. 'Solidary Individualism: The Moral Impact of Cultural Modernisation in Late Modernity', in *Risk, Environmnent and Modernity: Towards a New Ecology*, eds. Scott Lash and Bronislaw Szerszynski. London: Sage.

Bernstein, Henry. 2009. 'V.I. Lenin and A.V. Chayanov: Looking Back, Looking Forward', *The Journal of Peasant Studies: Critical Perspectives on Rural Politics and Development*, 36 (1).

Berry, Wendell. 1972/2004. *A Continuous Harmony: Essays Cultural and Agricultural*. New York: Harcourt Brace.

Bhalla, G.S. 2006. *Condition of Indian Peasantry*. New Delhi: National Book Trust.

Bhalla, G.S and Gurmail Singh. 2009. 'Economic Liberalisation and Indian Agriculture: A Statewise Analysis', *Economic and Political Weekly,* XLIV (52).

Bhaumik, Sankar Kumar. 2008. 'Introduction', in *Reforming Indian Agriculture: Towards Employment Generation and Poverty Reduction. Essays in Honour of G.K. Chadha,* ed. Sankar Kumar Bhaumik. New Delhi: Sage Publications.

Boehm, Christian. 2003. 'The Social Life of Fields: Labour Markets and Agrarian Change in Lesotho', *Paideusis-Journal for Interdisciplinary and Cross-Cultural Studies,* 3.

Brass, Tom. 1995. 'Introduction: The New Farmers' Movements in India', in *New Farmers' Movements in India,* ed.Tom Brass. London: Frank Cass and Co.

——. 2000. *Peasants, Populism, and Postmodernism: The Return of the Agrarian Myth.* London: Frank Cass and Co.

——. 2010. 'Class Dynamics of Agrarian Change: Writing a "Little Book on a Big Idea"' (MS). Paper presented at the Agrarian Studies Colloquium, Yale University.

Breman, Jan. 2007. *The Poverty Regime in Village India.* New Delhi: Oxford University Press.

Burawoy, Michael. 2002. 'Transition without Transformation: Russia's Involutionary Road to Capitalism', in *Locating Capitalism in Time and Space: Global Restructurings, Politics and Identity.* Stanford: Stanford University Press.

Butler, Judith. 2004. *Precarious Life: The Powers of Mourning and Violence.* London: Verso.

Cameron, Angus and Ronen Palan. 2004. *The Imagined Economies of Globalisation.* London: Sage Publications.

Centre for Environment and Food Security. 2002. *Field Report on Farmers' Suicide in Andhra Pradesh.* Hyderabad: CEFS.

Chand, Ramesh. 1999. 'Emerging Crisis in Punjab Agriculture: Severity and Options for Future', *Economic and Political Weekly,* 34 (13).

Chatterjee, Partha. 2009. 'Democracy and Economic Transformation in India', *Economic and Political Weekly*, 43 (16).

Chatterji, Angana P. 2009. *Violent Gods: Hindu Nationalism in India's Present. Narratives from Orissa.* New Delhi: Three Essays Collective.

Christian Aid. 2005. *The Damage Done: Aid, Death and Dogma*. (http://www.christianaid.org.uk/indeth/505caweek).

Citizens' Report.1998. *Gathering Agrarian Crisis: Farmers' Suicides in Warangal (AP).* MS. Hyderabad: Citizens Committee.

Cloke, P. 2005. 'Conceptualising Rurality', in *Handbook of Rural Studies*, eds. Cloke, P. and T.P. Marsden. London: Sage Publications.

Commission on Farmers' Welfare. 2005. Report Submitted to the Government of Andhra Pradesh. Hyderabad: Commission for Farmers' Welfare.

Corbridge Stuart and John Harriss. 2000. *Reinventing India: Liberalisation, Hindu Nationalism and Popular Democracy.* New Delhi: Oxford University Press.

Crook, Stephen. 1999. 'Ordering Risks', in *Risk and Sociocultural Theory: New Directions and Perspectives*, ed. Deborah Lipton. Cambridge: Cambridge University Press.

Comaroff, Jean and John Comaroff. 2001. *Millenium Capitalism and the Culture of Neoliberalism.* Durham: Duke University Press.

Communist Party of India (M). 2009. *Lies, Deceit, and Demagogy: The UPA Report Card on Agriculture.* New Delhi: CPI (M) Publications.

——. 2009. *Aam Aadmi Suffers in 'High Growth India': Bharat Nirman: New Deal or Raw Deal for Rural India?* New Delhi: CPI (M) Publications.

Dandekar, Ajay et al. 2005. *Causes of Farmer Suicides in Maharashtra: An Enquiry. Final Report Submitted to the Mumbai High Court.* Tata Institute of Social Sciences: Mumbai.

Dalla Costa, Maria Rosa. 2007. 'Reruralising the World', *The Commoner*, Issue 12. Summer. (www.thecommoner.org).

Datta, Pradip Kumar. 2008. *Nandigram and other Struggles: The Emergence of New Political Movements.* Kolkata: Gangchil.

Davis, Mike. 2001. *Late Victorian Holocausts: El Nino, Famines and the Making of the Third World.* London: Verso.

Denton, Robert Knox. 2000. 'This is Passion, and Where it Goes: Despair and Suicide among the Semai, a Non-violent People of West Malaysia', *Mousotus,* II.

Deshpande, Satish. 2003. *Contemporary India: A Sociological View.* New Delhi: Penguin.

Dev, Mahendra. 2004. 'How to Make Rural India Shine', *Economic and Political Weekly,* 34 (40).

Devi, Mahasweta. 1998. *Bitter Soil.* Kolkata: Seagull Books.

Douglas, Jack. 1966. 'Sociological Analysis of the Social Meanings of Suicide', *Archives of European Sociology,* Vol. VII.

——. 1967. *The Social Meanings of Suicide.* Princeton: Princeton University Press.

Dudley, Kathryn Marie. 2002. 'The Entrepreneurial Self: Identity and Morality in a Midwestern Farming Community', in *Fighting for the Farm: America Transformed,* ed. Jane Adams. Philadelphia: University of Pennsylvania.

Elias, Norbert. 1991. *The Society of Individuals,* ed. Michael Schroter. Trans. Edmund Jephcott. Oxford: Basil Blackwell.

Elson, Diane. 1998. 'The Economic, the Political and the Domestic: Businesses, States, and Households in the Organisation of Production', *New Political Economy,* 3 (2).

Elwin, Verrier. 1943. *Maria Murder and Suicide.* New Delhi: Oxford University Press.

Epstein, Scarlett. 2003. 'Forty Years of Change in Rural South India', *Journal of Social and Economic Development,* 5 (1).

Farmers' Commission of Experts and Vyavasayaranga Parikakshana. 2002. *Report of the Farmers' Commission of Experts on Agriculture in Andhra Pradesh.* Hyderabad: Navya Printers.

Fernandes, Walter. 2008. 'Paying the Price for Someone Else's Development', *InfoChange Agenda,* Issue 12.

Fullagar, Simone. 2003. 'Wasted Lives: The Social Dynamics of Shame and Youth Suicide', *Journal of Sociology*, 39 (3).

Gadgil, Sulochana. 2003. 'The Indian Monsoon and its Variability', *Annual Review of Earth Planet Sciences,* 31.

Gaikwad, Laxman. 1998. *Uchalya* (The Branded). Translated from Marathi by P.A. Kolharkar. New Delhi: Sahitya Akademi.

Galab, S.E. Revathi and P. Prudhvikar Reddy. 2009. 'Farmers' Suicides and Unfolding Agrarian Crisis in Andhra Pradesh', in *Agrarian Crisis in India,* eds. D. Narasimha Reddy and Srijit Mishra. New Delhi: Oxford University Press:

Galeano, Eduardo. 2009. *Mirrors: Stories of Almost Everyone.* London: Portobello Books.

Garikipati, S. 2009. 'Landless but Not Assetless: Female Agricultural Labour on the Road to Better Status, Evidence from India', *Journal of Peasant Studies*, 36 (3).

Geertz, Clifford. 1963. *Agricultural Involution.* Berkeley: University of California Press.

——. 2005. 'Agricultural Involution Revisited', in *The Anthropology of Development and Globalisation: From Classical Political Economy to Contemporary Neoliberalism*, eds. March Edelman and Angelique Haugerud. Massachusetts: Blackwell.

Ghosh, Jayati. 2004. 'The Rural Gloom', *Frontline,* December 3.

Giddens, Anthony. 1968. 'The Suicide Problem in French Sociology', *The British Journal of Sociology,* 16 (1).

Gidwani, Vinay. 2008. *Capital, Interrupted: Agrarian Development and the Politics of Work in India.* Minnesota: University of Minnesota Press.

Gill, Sucha Singh. 1995. 'Agrarian Capitalism and Political Processes in Punjab', in *Indian Agriculture in India since Independence*, ed. T.V. Satyamurthy. New Delhi: Oxford University Press.

——. 2004. 'Punjab Farmers' Movement: Continuity and Change', *Economic and Political Weekly*, 34 (27).

Gill, Anita and Lakwinder Singh. 2006. 'Farmers' Suicides and Response of Public Policy: Evidence, Diagnosis and Alternatives from Punjab', *Economic and Political Weekly*, 41 (26).

Gold, Ann. 2009. 'Tasteless Profits and Vexed Moralities: Assessments of the Present in Rural Rajasthan', *Journal of the Royal Anthropological Institute*, 15 (2).

Gorz, Andre. 1993. 'Political Ecology: Expertocracy versus Self-Limitation', *New Left Review*, I (202).

Government of India (GoI). 2006. *National Policy for Farmers*. New Delhi: Ministry of Agriculture.

——. 2007. *Report of the Expert Group on Agricultural Indebtedness*. New Delhi: Ministry of Finance.

——. 2008. *Agricultural Statistics at a Glance, 2008*. New Delhi: Academic Foundation.

Government of Karnataka. 2002. *Farmers' Suicides in Karnataka: A Scientific Analysis*. Bangalore: Office of the Expert Committee for Study on Farmers' Suicides.

Grover, D.K., Sanjay Kumar, and Kamal Vatta. 2008. 'Market Imperfections and Farmers' Distress in Punjab', in *Glimpses of Indian Agriculture: Macro and Micro Perspectives*, eds. R.S. Deshpande et al. New Delhi: Academic Publishers.

Gruere, Guillaume, Purvi Mehta-Bhatt, and Debdatta Sengupta. 2008. *Bt Cotton and Farmer Suicides in India*. Washington: International Food Policy Research Institute.

Gupta, Akhil. 1999. *Post-Colonial Developments: Agriculture in the Making of Modern India*. New Delhi: Oxford University Press.

Gupta, Dipankar. 2004. 'Whither the Indian Village? Culture and Agriculture in 'Rural' India'. Malcolm Adisheshiah Memorial Lecture. Chennai: Madras Institute of Development Studies.

Guruswamy, Mohan, Uma Natarajan and Shagun Khare. 2008. *The Crisis in Indian Agriculture: A Critical Study.* New Delhi: Hope India Publications.

Hardikar, Jaideep. 2008. 'CAG Report Slams Vidarbha Debt Waiver Package', *Indiatogether,* May 8 (www.indiatogether/org/2008/may/gov-theesri.html).

——. 2009. 'Inheritors of Debt and Distress' (countercurrents.org/hardikar.140209.htm).

Harriss-White, Barbara. 1999. 'Gender-Cleansing: The Paradox of Development and Deteriorating Female Life Chances in Tamil Nadu', in *Signposts: Gender Issues in Post-Independence India,* ed. Rajeswari Sundar Rajan. New Delhi: Kali for Women.

——. 2003. *India Working: Essays on Society and Economy.* Cambridge: Cambridge University Press.

Harriss-White, Barbara and S. Janakarajan. 2004. *Rural India Facing the Twenty-first Century: Essays on Long-term Village Change and Recent Development Policy.* London: Anthem Press.

Harriss, John. 2006. *Power Matters: Essays on Institutions, Politics, and Society in India.* New Delhi: Oxford University Press.

Harris, John, J. Jeyaranjan, K. Nagaraj. 2010. 'Land, Labour and Caste Politics in Rural Tamil Nadu in the Twentieth Century, Iruvelpattu (1916-2008)', *Economic and Political Weekly,* XLV (31).

Hobswawm, Eric. 1994. *The Age of Extremes.* New York: Pantheon Books.

Hudson, Martin. 2002. 'On the Dead of World History', *Race and Class,* 43(4).

Institute for Development Communication [IDC]. 1998. *Suicides in Punjab*. Chandigarh: Himalaya Press.

Indian Social Institute [ISI]. 2010. *Agriculture: Farmers' Suicides – Records and Documents from 1998-2000.* Compiled by K. Samu. Human Rights Documentation. New Delhi: Indian Statistical Institute (www.isiindia.org).

Indiresan, P.V. 2003. *Vision 2020: What India Can Be, and How to Make that Happen.* Hyderabad: ICFAI Books.

Iyer, Gopal and M.S. Manick. 2000. *Indebtedness, Impoverishment and Suicides in Rural Punjab.* Delhi: Indian Publishers.

Jaffrelot, Christophe and Sanjay Kumar. 2009. *Rise of the Plebeians? The Changing Face of Indian Legislative Assemblies.* New Delhi: Routledge.

Jaworski, Katrina. 2010. 'The Author, Agency, and Suicide', *Social Identities*, 16 (5).

Jeffrey, Craig and Jens Lerche. 2000. 'Dimensions of Dominance: Class and State in Uttar Pradesh', in *The Everyday State and Society in Modern India*, eds. C.J. Fuller and Vernonique Benei. New Delhi: Social Science Press.

Jodha, N.S. 2001. *Life on the Edge: Sustaining Agriculture and Community Resources in Fragile Environments.* New Delhi: Oxford University Press.

Jodhka, Surinder. 2005. 'Beyond 'Crises': Rethinking Contemporary Punjab Agriculture', Working Paper 4. GAPS series. Hyderabad: Centre for Economics and Social Sciences.

——. 2008. 'The Decline of Agriculture', in *Reforming Indian Agriculture: Towards Employment Generation and Poverty Reduction. Essays in Honour of G.K. Chadha*, ed. S.K. Bhaumik. New Delhi: Sage Publications.

John, Mary, et al. 2009. 'Dispensing with Daughters: Technology, Society, Economy in North India', *Economic and Political Weekly*, XLIV (15).

John, Mary. 2010. 'Reflections on Marginality'. Keynote Presentation at the XXXIV Indian Academy of Social Sciences Congress, Guwahati, Dec 29.

Kakkar, Sudhir. 1997. *Colours of Violence.* New Delhi: Viking.

Kalam, Abdul A.P.J. (with Y.S.Rajan). 1998. *India 2020: A Vision for the New Millenium.* New Delhi: Penguin Books.

Kamble, Shantabai. 1992. 'Naja Goes to School and Doesn't', in *A Corpse in the Well.* Translations from Marathi Dalit Autobiographies, ed. Arjun Damle. Hyderabad: Disha Books.

Kashipur Solidarity Group. 2008. *A Sinking Feeling: Behind the Acute Water Crisis in Bundelkhand.* New Delhi: Kashipur Solidarity Group.

Kasperon, J.X. and R.E. Kasperon. 2001. *Global Environmental Risk.* Tokyo: Earth Scan/UNU Press.

Karulkar, R.P. 2006. *Farmers' Suicides in Marathwada Region of Maharashtra: A Report.* Aurangabad: Swami Ramanand Teerth Marathwada Research Institute.

Kaur, Ravinder. 2008. 'Dispensable Daughters and Bachelor Sons: Sex Discrimination in North India', *Economic and Political Weekly,* XLIII (30).

Khilnani, Sunil. 1997. *The Idea of India.* London: Penguin.

Kingfisher, Catherine and J. Muskovsky. 2008. 'The Limits of Neoliberalism', *Critique of Anthropology,* 28(2).

Krishna, Anirudh. 2003. 'What is Happening to Caste? A View from Some North Indian Villages, *The Journal of Asian Studies,* 62 (4).

Krishnaraj, Maithreyi and Aruna Kanchi. 2008. *Women Farmers of India.* New Delhi: National Book Trust.

Kumar, Richa. 2009. *The Yellow Revolution in Malwa: Alternative Arenas of Struggle and the Cultural Politics of Development.* (MS) Ph.D Dissertation. Science, Technology, and Society Program. Submitted to Massachusetts Institute of Technology, Massachusetts.

Kumbamu, Ashok. 2009. 'The Global Knowledge Encounter: A Sociological Analysis of the Introduction of Genetically Modified Seeds in Warangal, India', *International Social Science Journal,* 60 (195).

Kundu, Amitabh. 2006. 'Globalisation, Inequality and the Mobility of Populations in India', in *Contested Transformations: Changing Economies and Identities in Contemporary India,* eds. John, Mary, Praveen Jha and Surinder Jodhka. Tulika: New Delhi.

Latour, Bruno. 2007. *Reassembling the Social: An Introduction to Actor-Network Theory.* New York: Oxford University Press.

Lefebvre, Henri. 1991. *The Production of Space.* Trans. Donald Nicholson-Smith. Oxford: Blackwell.

Lipton, Deborah.1999. Ed. *Risk and Sociocultural Theory: New Directions and Perspectives.* Cambridge: Cambridge University Press.

Livingston, Julie. 2009. 'Suicide, Risk, and Investment in the Heart of the African Miracle', *Cultural Anthropology,* 24(4).

Ludden, David. 1985. *Peasant History in South India.* Princeton: Princeton University Press.

——. 1992. 'India's Development Regime' in *Colonialism and Culture,* ed. Nicholas Dirks. Ann Arbor: University of Michigan Press.

Macdonald, Charles J-H. 2003. 'Urug: An Anthropological Investigation on Suicide in the Palawan,Philippines', *SouthEast Asian Studies,* 40(4).

Madhuvanti. 2007. *Agrarian Distress in Vidarbha.* Pune: YASHADA.

Madsen, Stig Toft. 2001. Coconut Toddy, Chewing Tobacco and Genetically Modified Cotton: Moral Choices for a Farmers' Association in India. MS.

Malamoud, Charles.1996. 'The Theology of Debt in Brahmanism', in *Cooking the World: Ritual and Thought in Ancient India.* Translated from the French by David White. New Delhi: Oxford University Press.

Mamdani, Mahmood. 2001. 'Beyond Settler and Native Political Identities: Overcoming the Political Legacy of Colonialism', *Comparative Studies in Society and History,* 43 (4).

Mayer, Peter (with Clare Bradley, Della Steen and Teherah Zianian). 2011. *Suicide and Society in India.* New Delhi: Routledge.

Meeta and Rajivlochan. 2006. *Farmers' Suicide: Facts and Possible Interventions.* Pune: YASHADA.

Michelluti, Lucia. 2008. *Vernacularisation of Democracy: Politics, Caste and Religion in India.* Delhi: Routledge.

Mines, Diane P. and Nicholas Yazgi. 2010. *Village Matters: Relocating Villages in the Contemporary Anthropology of India*. New Delhi: Oxford University Press.

Mishra, Banikanta. 2010. 'Agriculture, Industry and Mining in Orissa in the Post-Liberalisation Era: An Inter-District and Inter-State Panel Analysis', *Economic and Political Weekly*, XLV (20).

Mishra, Srijit. 2006. *Suicides of Farmers in Maharashtra*. Mumbai: Indira Gandhi Institute of Development Research.

Mody, Utpala. 2007. 'Samlekhana is a Step Towards Self-Realisation' (MS). Paper presented at the National Seminar on Bioethics. Mumbai.

Mohanakumar, S. and R.K. Sharma. 2006. 'Analysis of Farmers' Suicides in Kerala', *Economic and Political Weekly*, 41(16).

Mohanty, B.B. and Sangeetha Shroff. 2004. 'Farmers' Suicides in Maharashtra', *Economic and Political Weekly*, 32(54).

Mohanty, B.B. 2005. '"We are Like the Living Dead": Farmer Suicides in Maharashtra, Western India', *The Journal of Peasant Studies*, 32(2).

Nagaraj, D.R. 1998. 'Beyond the Essentialist and Constructivist Paradigms: Notes on Indian Pluralism' (MS).

Nagaraj, K. 2008. 'Farmers' Suicides in India: Magnitude, Trends and Spatial Patterns' (MS). Chennai: Madras Institute of Development Studies.

Nair, R.N. and Vineetha Menon. 2009. 'Distress Debt and Suicides among Agrarian Households: Findings from Village Studies in Kerala', in *Agrarian Crisis in India*, eds. D. Narasimha Reddy and Srijit Mishra. New Delhi: Oxford University Press.

National Commission for Farmers (NCF). 2006. *Serving Farmers and Saving Farming*. New Delhi: Ministry of Agriculture.

National Crime Records Bureau (NCRB). 2008. *Accidental Deaths and Suicides in India: 1997-2006*. New Delhi: Ministry of Home Affairs.

NABARD. 2008. *Action Plan to Address Agrarian Distress in India*. New Delhi: NABARD.

National Sample Survey Organisation (NSSO). 2005a. 'Situation Assessment Survey of Farmers': Reports no. 496, 498, 499. Ministry of Statistics and Programme Implementation: New Delhi: Government of India.

——. 2005b. 'Rural Labour Enquiry Report on Indebtedness among Rural Labour Households', 55th Round. 1999-2000. Ministry of Statistics and Programme Implementation. New Delhi: Government of India.

Nayyar, Rohini and Alakh N. Sharma. 2005. *Rural Transformation in India: The Role of Non-Farm Sector.* New Delhi: Manohar Publications.

Newman, Brian. 2007. 'Bitter Harvest: Farmer Suicide and the Unforeseen Social, Environmental and Economic Impacts of the Green Revolution in Punjab, India'. Development Report no. 15. California: Food First: Institute for Food and Development Policy.

Omvedt, Gail. 1992. 'Capitalist Agriculture and Rural Classes in India', in *Class, State and Development in India,* ed. Berch Berberroglu. New Delhi: Sage Publications.

Ong, Aihwa. 1999. *Flexible Citizenship: The Cultural Logics of Transnationality.* Durham: Duke University Press.

Padhi, Ranjana. 2009. 'On Women Surviving Farmer Suicides in Punjab', *Economic and Political Weekly,* XLIV (19).

Paine, Tom. 2009/1797. *Agrarian Justice.* New Edition. London: Joshua Allen.

Pallavi, Aparna. 2007. 'Land Titles Don't Come Easy for Farm Widows', (http://www.womenenvironment.org/detail.php?pageId=806).

Palshikar, Sanjay. 2010. 'Understanding Humiliation', in *Humiliation: Claims and Context,* ed.Gopal Guru. New Delhi: Oxford University Press.

Panini, M.N. 1998. 'Trends in Cultural Globalisation: From Agriculture to Agri-Business', *Economic and Politial Weekly,* 34(31).

Patnaik, Utsa. 2004. 'External Trade, Domestic Employment and Food Security: Recent Outcomes of Neo-Liberal Economic Reforms' (MS). Paper Presented at the Conference on 'The Question of Asia in the New Global Order', Duke University.

——. 2006, 'Unleashing the Market: Global Capitalism, Deflation and Agrarian Crisis in Developing Countries', in *Contested Transformations: Changing Economies and Identities in Contemporary India*, eds. Mary John et al. New Delhi: Tulika Press.

Perspectives. 2009. *Harvesting Despair: Agrarian Crisis in India.* New Delhi: Perspectives.

Pinto, Vivek. 1998. *Gandhi's Vision and Values. The Moral Quest for Change in Indian Agriculture.* New Delhi: Sage Publications.

Prasad, Purendra. 2003. 'Rights of Farmers in the Context of Suicides in Andhra Pradesh', *Indian Journal of Human Rights*, 7 (1-2).

Ramachandran, V.K. and Madhura Swaminathan. 2005. 'Introduction', in *Financial Liberalisation and Rural Credit in India.* New Delhi: Tulika.

Ramirez-Ferrero, Eric. 2005. *Troubled Fields: Men, Emotions, and the Crisis in American Farming.* New York: Columbia University Press.

Rana, R.P. 2006. 'Was there an Agrarian Crisis in Mughal North India During the Late Seventeenth and Early Eighteenth Centuries?', *Social Scientist*, 34.

Rao, C.H. Hanumantha. 2005. *Agriculture, Food Security, Poverty, and Environment: Essays on Post-Reform India.* New Delhi: Oxford University Press.

Rao, Kalipatnam Rama. 2006. *Yagnam and Other Stories.* Translated from Telugu by C.L.L. Jayaprada. New Delhi: Sahitya Academi.

Rao, G. Niranjan and K. Narayan Nair. 2003. 'Change and Transformation in Rural South India: Findings from Village Studies', *Economic and Political Weekly, 38 (32).*

Rao, G. Niranjan and D. Narasimha Reddy. 2010. *Rural Transformation: Perspectives from Village Studies in Andhra Pradesh.* Delhi: Daanish Books.

Rao, V.M. and D.V. Gopalappa. 2004. 'Agricultural Growth and Farmer Distress: Tentative Perspectives from Karnataka', *Economic and Political Weekly*, 32(54).

Reddy, Narasimha D. and Srijit Mishra. 2008. 'Crisis in Agriculture and Rural Distress in Post-Reform India', in *India Development Report, 2008*, ed. R. Radhakrishna. New Delhi: Oxford University Press.

——. 2009. 'Agriculture in the Reforms Regime', in *Agrarian Crisis in India*, eds. D. Narasimha Reddy and Srijit Mishra. New Delhi: Oxford University Press.

Reserve Bank of India (RBI). 2006. *Report of the Working Group to Suggest Measures to Assist Distressed Farmers*. Mumbai: Reserve Bank of India.

Revati, E. and R.V. Ramana Murthy. 2005. *Changing Seed Policy, Law and Regulation: An Appraisal of the Emerging Seed Markets in Andhra Pradesh*. GAPS Series: Working Paper 6. Hyderabad: Centre for Economic and Social Studies.

Richards, Paul. 1993. 'Knowledge or Performance?', in *An Anthropological Critique of Development: The Growth of Ignorance*, ed. M. Hobart. London: Routledge.

Robb, Peter. 1996. 'Variant Meanings of Agriculture: Implications for Research and Policy', in *Meanings of Agriculture: Essays in South Asian History and Economics*, ed. Peter Robb. New Delhi: Oxford University Press.

Rustin, Michael. 1994. 'Incomplete Modernity: Ulrich Beck's Risk Society', *Radical Philosophy*, 67 (Summer).

Rutten, Mario. 1995. *Farms and Factories. Social Profile of Large Farmers and Rural Industrialists in West India*. New Delhi: Oxford University Press.

Ruud, Arild Engelsen. 2000. 'Talking Dirty About Politics: A View From a Bengali Village', in *The Everyday State and Society in Modern India*, eds., C.J. Fuller and Vernonique Benei. New Delhi: Social Science Press.

Ruzicka, Lado T. 1998. 'Suicide in Countries and Areas of the ESCAP Region', *Asia-Pacific Population Journal*, Vol. 13, No. 4, December(www.unescap.org/appj.asp).

Sainath, P. 2007a. 'Striking a Note of Dissent', *The Hindu*, January 27.

——. 2007b. 'The Farm Crisis: Why Have Over One Lakh Farmers Killed Themselves in the Past Decade?' Speaker's Lecture Series: Parliament House, New Delhi. September 6.

——. 2009. 'Maharashtra: The Dull Days of White Gold', *The Hindu*, April 3.

——. 2010. 'Farm Suicides: a 12-year saga', *India Together*, February 4.

Sarma, E.A.S. 2004. 'Is Rural Economy Breaking Down? Farmers' Suicides in Andhra Pradesh', *Economic and Political Weekly*, 34(28).

Sanyal, Kalyan. 2008. *Rethinking Capitalist Development: Primitive Accumulation, Governmentality, and Post-Colonial Capitalism*. New Delhi: Routledge.

Schlesinger, Lee. 2010. 'Arms and the World: Village Apshinge (Maharashtra) Bounding and Extending Where', in *Village Matters: Relocating Villages in the Contemporary Anthropology of India*, eds. Diane Mines and Nicholas Yazgi. New Delhi: Oxford University Press.

Scott, James. 1998. *Seeing Like a State: How Certain Schemes to Improve the Human Condition Have Failed*. New Haven: Yale University Press.

Sen, Abhijit and M.S. Bhatia. 2004. *Cost of Cultivation and Farm Income. State of the Indian Farmer: A Millenium Study*. New Delhi: Academic Foundation.

Shah, Mihir, Rangu Rao and P.S. Vijay Shankar. 2007. 'Rural Credit in 20th Century India: An Overview of History and Perspectives', *Economic and Political Weekly*, 42 (15).

Shah, Mihir. 2009. 'Structures of Power in Indian Society: A Response', *Economic and Political Weekly*, 43(46).

——. 2010. 'The Power of Uncertainty: Reflections on the Nature of Transformational Initiatives', *Economic and Political Weekly*, 45 (25).

Shanin, Theodor. 2009. 'Chayanov's Triple Death and Tenuous Resurrection: An Essay About Understanding, About Roots of Plausibility and About Rural Russia', *The Journal of Peasant Studies: Critical Perspectives on Rural Politics and Development*, 36 (1).

Sheridan, Cormac. 2009. 'Doubts Surround Link between Bt Cotton Failure and Farmer Suicide', *Nature Biotechnology, 29(9-10)*(http://www.nature.com/nbt/journal/v27/n1/full/nbt0109-9.html).

Shivaramaiah, Prof. 2007. *Kathi Yavaduadhare Yeenu? (Does it Matter Which is the Knife?)*. Bangalore: Karnataka Rajya Raitha Sangha and Hasiru Sene.

Sharma, Devinder. 2006. 'Indian Villages for Sale', www.countercurrents.org/gl-sharma130206.htm.

Shiva, Vandana and A.H. Jafri. 1998. *Seeds of Suicide: The Ecological and Human Costs of Globalisation of Agriculture*. New Delhi: Research Foundation for Science, Technology and Ecology.

Shiva, Vandana. 1991. *The Violence of the Green Revolution: Third World Agriculture, Ecology and Politics*. Malaysia: Third World Network.

Siddiqi, Asiya. 1973. *Agrarian Change in a Northern State, U.P. 1819-1833*. Oxford: Clarendon Press.

Singh, K.S. 2001. 'Ecology, Identity and Culture', *The Human Landscape*: IIC Quarterly, Winter 2000 and Spring.

Singh, Sukhpal. 2006. 'Credit, Indebtedness and Farmer Suicides: Some Missing Links', *Economic and Political Weekly*, XLI (26).

Singh, Surjit. 2007. 'Economic Diversification: Some Reflections from Experience', *The Indian Journal of Labour Economics*, 50(4).

——. 2008. 'Agricultural Risks and Public Policy: Cross Country Experiences', in *Reforming Indian Agriculture: Towards Employment Generation and Poverty Reduction. Essays in Honour of G.K. Chadha*, ed. S.K. Bhaumik. New Delhi: Sage Publications.

Sivaramakrishnan, K. and Arun Agrawal. 2003. *Regional Modernities: The Cultural Politics of Development in India*. Stanford: Stanford University Press.

Sriram, M.S. 2008. 'Agrarian Distress and Rural Credit: Peeling the Onion', in *State of India's Livelihoods: The 4P Report*, ed. Shankar Datta and Vipin Sharma. New Delhi: Access Development Services.

Srivastava, Ravi. 2005. 'India: Internal Migration Links with Poverty and Development' (MS). Paper presented at the Regional Conference on Migration and Development in Asia, Lanzou, China.

Stokes, Eric.1978. *The Peasant and the Raj: Studies in Agrarian Society and Peasant Rebellion in Colonial India.* Delhi: Vikas Publishing.

Stone, Glenn D. 2007a. 'Agricultural Deskilling and the Spread of Genetically Modified Cotton in Warangal', *Current Anthropology,* 48 (1).

——. 2007b. 'The Birth and Death of Traditional Knowledge: Paradoxical Effects of Biotechnology in India', in *Biodiversity and the Law: Intellectual Property, Biotechnology, and Traditional Knowledge,* ed. Charles McManis. London: EarthScan.

Suri, K.C. 2006. 'Political Economy of Agrarian Distress', *Economic and Political Weekly,* 41 (6).

Swift, Richard. 2007. 'Death by Cotton', *New Internationalist,* 399.

Tanabe, Akio. 2007. 'Toward Vernacular Democracy: Moral Social Society and Post-Postcolonial Transformation in Rural India', *American Ethnologist,* 34 (3).

Tandon, Raj. 2002. *Primary Education and Panchayat Raj Institutions.* New Delhi: PRIA.

Taylor, Gabriele. 1985. *Pride, Shame and Guilt: Emotions of Self-Assessment.* Oxford: Clarendon Press.

Tejaswi, Poornachandra. 2006. *Mayaloka: I (World of Illusions).* Mysore: Pustaka Prakashana.

Thakur, Manish. 2006. 'Indian Village: Revisiting the Problematic'. Paper presented at the National Seminar on 'Understanding Agrarian Change in India: Challenges for Theory and Method' (MS). March 2-3. University of Hyderabad.

Thakur, Upendra. 1963. *The History of Suicide in India: An Introduction.* Delhi: Munshi Ram Manohar Lal.

Thorner, Daniel. 1972. *The Agrarian Prospect in India.* Delhi: Allied Publishers.

Tilly, Charles. 2008. *Explaining Social Processes.* London: Paradigm Publishers.

Toxics Link. 2002. *The Killing Fields: Farmer Deaths Due to Exposure to Pesticides in Warangal District.* New Delhi: Toxics Link.

Upadhya, Carol. 1997. 'Social and Cultural Strategies of Class Formation in Coastal Andhra Pradesh', *Contributions to Indian Sociology*, 31 (2).

Vakulabharanam, Vamsi. 2005. 'Growth and Distress in a South Indian Peasant Economy During the Era of Economic Liberalisation', *The Journal Of Development Studies,* 41(6).

——. 2010. 'Does Class Matter? Class Structure and Worsening Inequality in India', *Economic and Political Weekly,* XLV (29).

Vaidyanathan, A. 2006. 'Farmers' Suicides and the Agrarian Crisis', *Economic and Political Weekly*, 41(38).

Van der Ploeg, Jan Douwe. 2010. 'The Peasantries of the Twenty-First Century: The Commoditisation Debate Revisited', *Journal of Peasant Studies,* 37 (1).

Vasavi, A.R. 1999. 'Agrarian Distress in Bidar: Market, State and Suicides', *Economic and Political Weekly,* 34 (32).

——. 2004. 'Field Notes on Suicides by Agriculturists: Mandya and Hassan Districts' (MS).

——. 2009. 'Suicides and the Making of India's Agrarian Distress', *South African Review of Sociology*, 40 (1).

Veiga, José Eli da. 2004. 'The Rural Dimension of Brasil', *Estudos Sociedade e Agricultura*, 12 (1).

Venkateshwarlu, Davuluri. 1998. *Cotton Farmers' Suicides in Andhra Pradesh.* Report Submitted to Basix. Hyderabad: Basix Publications.

Vepa, Swarna S. 2009. *Bearing the Brunt: Impact of Rural Distress on Women.* New Delhi: Sage Publications.

Vijaya Times. 2006. 'Suicide by Farmers Averted in Mysore', August 18.

Vijaybhaskar, M. 2010. 'Saving Agricultural Labour from Agriculture: SEZs and Politics of Silence in Tamil Nadu', *Economic and Political Weekly*, XLV (6)

Vikas Samvaad, 2008, '*M.P mai Phansi ke Phande par Jhulte Kisaan*' (M.P's agriculturists: Hanging in the Gallows). Report. Bhopal: Vikas Samvaad.

Visvanathan, Shiv. 1997. *A Carnival for Science*. New Delhi: Oxford University Press.

Vyas, V.S. 2004. 'Agrarian Distress: Strategies to Protect Vulnerable Sections', *Economic and Political Weekly*, 32 (54).

Walker, Kathy Le Mons. 2008. 'Neoliberalism on the Ground in Rural India: Predatory Growth, Agrarian Crisis, Internal Colonization, and the Intensification of Class Struggle', *The Journal of Peasant Studies*, 35(4).

White, Benjamin.1983. 'Agricultural Involution and its Critics: Twenty Years Later', *Bulletin of Concerned Asian Scholars*, 15 (2).

World Health Organisation. 2000. *Preventing Suicides: A Resource Guide for Media Professionals*. Department of Mental Health. Geneva: World Health Organisation.

Zachariah, Anand. 2010. 'Rethinking Organophosphate Poisoning/ Suicide in India', in *Towards a Critical Medical Practice: Reflections on the Dilemmas of Medical Culture Today*, eds. Anand Zachariah, R. Srivatsan and Susie Tharu. Hyderabad: Orient Blackswan.

Acknowledgement

This book and the ideas in it have been incubated, amongst other work, since 1998 and have now found expression as a way to understand the historic and significant changes that rural India is undergoing. For encouraging me to persist working on agrarian issues (despite the fact that it is not on the list of fashionable social science topics and themes), even as I was preoccupied with other projects, I thank Professors Virendra Kumar, M.N. Panini, Anand Chakravarti, and Uma Chakravarti. To Lee Schlesinger of Ann Arbor, Michigan, is owed much. His detailed comments on the first paper and then his incisive and critical comments and suggestions at the penultimate version of this book have been central to finalizing the book. My inability to incorporate or attend to all his suggestions has only made the book poorer. My gratitude is also to Padmini Swaminathan, Mary John, M.S. Sriram, Sreedevi Lakshmikutty, and Janaki Nair who reviewed the full manuscript at short notice and helped fine-tune it. K. Sivaramakrishnan and Mahesh Rangarajan provided pertinent comments that enabled me to elaborate on the drawbacks of the Green Revolution and elucidate the conditions of individual agriculturists. Several persons were generous with their time, ideas, and materials and shared them with me over the internet. Among them were: Kalyan Sanyal of Calcutta University who took the trouble to respond to my rather naïve queries over the email. Special thanks to P. Sainath for so generously sharing a copy of Shri Raut's suicide note and to Shivali Tukdeo for translating it. Sachin Jain of Vikas Samvaad, Bhopal, and Shubhranshu Choudhury of Chhattisgarh's CGnet generously shared their materials with me, thereby filling in some details for the states of Madhya Pradesh and Chhattisgarh. Julie Livingston shared her material on suicides in Botswana, Barbara Harriss-White responded to queries and provided copies of reports, Kathryn Marie Dudley took the trouble to share an inaccessible essay with me, and Glen Stone pointed out some technical details pertaining to agriculture. Vinay Gidwani read a draft of an early version of some chapters and provided incisive and critical comments. Shri Veersangaiah, secretary of the Karnataka Rajya Raitha Sangha, shared his views, angst and writings on agrarian issues with me. Rita Ratnam, Erach Bharucha, Amarlal Kalro, Carol Upadhya, Dilip Ahuja, Rachel Schurman, Michael Goldman, Pulapre Balakrishnan, D.D. Nampoothiri and Parvathi Menon have provided enduring support and friendship and I hope this book is a small token of my gratitude to them. Vanaja Ramprasad, Sunita Rao, Pandurang Hegde, Sangita Sharma, and Devinder Sharma are now friends whose commitment to addressing the entrenched problems of agriculture and biodiversity have provided the hope that is required in seeking to address the many travails of India's agriculture and rural societies.

Elizabeth Louis, as she conducted her field work in Andhra Pradesh, shared her experiences and data and enabled me to engage with contemporary trends in agrarian issues. Tara Sinha, long-time friend, lent a hand by tracing Shri Jhala and accessing his materials on suicides in Gujarat. Thanks are to Sarah Joseph, Kala Sunder, Sibaji Bandopadhyay, R. Sunder, Vishalakshi Padmanabhan, Sangeetha Kamat, Biju Mathew, G.S. Jayadeva, H.D. Prashanth, Chandan Gowda, Sham Kashyap, Arvind Susarla, Deepti Priya Mehrotra, Supriya Roy Chowdhury, Ann Gold, Anita Gill, Thomas Weisskopf, Peter Van der Veer and Andrew Willford for their intellectual and social support.

Anwar Jafri, R.N. Syag, and Dhuleshwar Raut of Samavesh, and Anjali Noronha of Eklavya, Madhya Pradesh have shared their experiences of rural Madhya Pradesh with me and I thank them and the team at Samavesh for making possible my visits to Khategaon and the villages in the Dewas area. Michele Pimbert and P. V. Satheesh have helped scaffold my interest in agrarian issues and through their organisation of the *Raitha Theerpu* (Farmers' Jury) have facilitated a sharing of some of these ideas with agriculturists from Karnataka.

My erstwhile colleagues P. Veerbhadranaika, B. Shivnanja, C. Veerendra, and Lakshamma from the Vidyankura project in Chamarajnagar, Karnataka, have often discussed their own lives and the challenges of living in rural areas with me and I am grateful to them for their interest, generosity, and support. The writings and work of James Scott, David Ludden, Susan George, Jan Breman, Wendell Berry, and Barbara Harriss-White have been guide posts to my interest in rural and agrarian issues and I would like to record my appreciation for their efforts and insights. Prof. Trent Schroyer, as a visitor to Bangalore during the summers of 2007-09, provided both intellectual and moral support to pursue a deeper study of issues related to the condition of rural India and to discern its own trajectory. I am grateful to him and for his ideas represented in his critique of the dominant neo-classical economic paradigms and their associated socio-cultural configurations. To Prof. Diane Elson is owed the section on focusing on household and family level capability decline and I thank her for her interest and support.

Early versions and ideas for this manuscript were presented at seminars and lectures at various institutions: at Nagarjuna University, organised by CESS, Hyderabad (2005) by K. C. Suri and others; at the University of Hyderabad during the seminar organised by Purendra Prasad (2006); at the Centre for Rural Studies, Lal Bahadur Shastri National Academy for Administration, Mussorie (2007); and at the Department of Development Studies, Kannada University, Hampi as part of the Visiting Faculty lecture series organised by H.D. Prashanth (2009). An early version of this was presented at my former institution, National Institute for Advanced Studies, Bangalore. An essay, 'Suicides and the Making of India's Agrarian Distress' was read by members of the Agrarian Studies Program at Yale University and I thank Prof. James Scott and K. Sivaramakrishnan for making the presentation there possible and for all the sharp questions (only some of which have I been able to answer in this book). I am also grateful to all the participants at the Yale seminar for their engaged and concerned queries and feedback.

To my friends in Madbhavi village, Bijapur, I owe special and long term gratitude for sharing their experiences and views on agriculture with me. In facilitating a revisit study in 2009 and sharing their experiences, they reinforced my view that the problem with India's agriculture is its structural bases and not its knowledge forms. To my mother, H.P. Lakshmidevamma, whose critical commentary on the deterioration of rural and agricultural life has buttressed my own views, I owe gratitude for forbearance and support. My own unpaid debt is to all the agriculturists who I met, interviewed and discussed issues with. And as a small way to repay these personal debtsto those whose problems I was unable to alleviate, I donate the royalties from the sale of this book to the organisation Vanastree (based in Sirsi, Karnataka), for utilisation in their programmes to promote and support seed-saving, organic and cooperative agriculture.

Funds for research assistance were made available through the Reserve Bank of India supported programme on 'Interdisciplinary Approaches to Economic Issues', which is housed at NIAS, and I thank Poornima and Rachel Mathew for their research assistance over two months. The final touches to the manuscript, much delayed over the years, were made during a three-month fellowship at the Indian Institute of Advanced Studies, Shimla. I thank the Director, Prof. Peter deSouza, for his support and all the fellows who engaged with the presentation made at the institute. For taking extra interest in this issue, and being true fellows at the IIAS, I would like to thank P. Narayanan, Anita Cherian, Sanjay Palshikar, Mohinder Singh, and Sowmyabrata Chowdhury. Sarojini Thakur, a friend from and of the Himalayas, provided both hospitality and intellectual support in Shimla and I am grateful to her for her encouragement. Finally, to National Institute of Advanced Studies, Bangalore, I owe gratitude and to its excellent support staff, Sheela Venkatesh, Srinivas Aithal, A. Devaraju, K.S. Ramakrishna, Vijayalakshmi, Stella, Sandhya, Gayathri Lokande, Shashi and Ramesh for helping run an efficient organisational set-up. And, to an exemplary student, Revathi Kumaran for help in editing the final version. A new set of colleagues from the 'Network for Rural and Agrarian Studies' now provide additional impetus and support to engage in such work; and I wish to acknowledge their contributions and interest.

Much gratitude is owed to Asad Zaidi and Nalini Taneja of Three Essays Collective, who consented to publishing this work after reviewing only an essay and for bearing with the long delay in submitting this manuscript to them.

Bangalore
2012

A.R. Vasavi

INDEX

Three Essays Collective focuses on works of scholarship which touch upon issues of contemporary concern. They address a wide range of themes in history, society, politics, culture, education and the media. South Asian themes predominate in, but do not exhaust, the scope of these publications. They are intended to familiarise readers with current debates in their respective fields, even as they enlarge areas of enquiry.

Three Essays
COLLECTIVE

❖

OTHER TITLES

Aijaz Ahmad, *On Communalism and Globalisation: Offensives of the Far Right*

Amar Farooqi, *Opium City: The Making of Early Victorian Bombay*

Angana Chatterji, *Violent Gods: Hindu Nationalism in India's Present – Narratives from Orissa*

Antoinette Burton, *Brown Over Black: Race and the Politics of Postcolonial Citation*

Archana Prasad, *Against Ecological Romanticism: Verrier Elwin and the Making of an Anti-Modern Tribal Identity*

Arup Banerji, *Old Routes: North Indian Nomads and Bankers in Afghan, Uzbek and Russian Lands*

Ashraf Aziz, *Light of the Universe: Essays on Hindustani Film Music*

Barbara Harriss-White, *India's Market Society: Three Essays in Political Economy*

Biswamoy Pati, *Identity, Hegemony, Resistance: Towards a Social History of Conversions in Orissa, 1800-2000*

Brinda Karat, *Survival and Emancipation: Notes from Indian Women's Struggles*

Colin Leys, *Total Capitalism: Market Politics, Market State*

Eduardo Galeano, *Open Veins of Latin America: Five Centuries of the Pillage of a Continent*

Jackie Assayag and Véronique Bénéï (eds.), *Re-mapping Knowledge: The Making of South Asian Studies in India, Europe and America, 19th-20th centuries*

John S Saul, *Development After Globalisation: Theory and Practice for an Embattled South in a New Imperial Age*

John S Saul, *Decolonisation and Empire: Contesting the Rhetoric and Practice of Resubordination in Southern Africa and Beyond*

John S Saul, *Liberation Lite: The Roots of Recolonisation in Southern Africa*

KN Panikkar, *An Agenda for Cultural Action and Other Essays*

Kristoffel Lieten, *Views on Development: The Local and the Global in India and Pakistan*

Madhu Trivedi, *The Emergence of the Hindustani Tradition: Music, Dance and Drama in North India, 13th to 19th Centuries*

Meera Nanda, *Breaking the Spell of Dharma and Other Essays*

Meera Nanda, *The Wrongs of the Religious Right: Reflections on Science, Secularism and Hindutva*

Meeto (Kamaljit Bhasin-Malik), *In the Making: Identity Formation in South Asia*

Mukul Dube, *The Path of the Parivar: Articles on Gujarat and Hindutva*

Omar Khalidi, *Khaki and Ethnic Violence in India: Army, Police and Paramilitary Forces during Communal Riots*

Omar Khalidi, *Muslims in Indian Economy*

Paul R Brass, *Forms of Collective Violence: Riots, Pogroms, and Genocide in Modern India*

Patricia Jeffery and Roger Jeffery, *Confronting Saffron Demography: Religion, Fertility, and Women's Status in India*

Pritam Singh, *Economy, Culture and Human Rights: Turbulence in Punjab, India and Beyond*

Radhika Desai, *Slouching Towards Ayodhya: From Congress to Hindutva in Indian Politics*

Ralph Russell, *Findings, Keepings: The Autobiography of Ralph Russell, Early Years, 1918-1945*

Ralph Russell, *Losses Gains: The Autobiography of Ralph Russell, Middle Years, 1945-1958*

RK Jain, *Indian Transmigrants: Malaysian and Comparative Essays*

Romila Thapar, *The Aryan: Recasting Constructs*

S. Irfan Habib, *To Make the Deaf Hear: Ideology and Programme of Bhagat Singh and His Comrades*

Shereen Ratnagar, *The Other Indians: Essays on Pastoralists and Pre-Historic Tribal People*

Shubh Mathur, *The Everyday Life of Hindu Nationalism: An Ethnographic Account*

Subhash Gatade, *The Saffron Condition: Politics of Repression and Exclusion in Neoliberal India*

Sunil Kumar, *The Present in Delhi's Pasts: Five Essays*

Sunil Kumar (ed.), *Demolishing Myths or Mosques and Temples: Readings on History and Temple Desecration in Medieval India*

Utsa Patnaik, *The Republic of Hunger and Other Essays*

Vasudha Dalmia, *Orienting India: European Knowledge Formation in the Eighteenth and Nineteenth Centuries*

Vijay Prashad, *The American Scheme: Three Essays*

Vina Mazumdar, *The Mind and the Medium: Explorations in the Evolution of British Imperial Policy in India*

Zaheer Baber, *Secularism, Communalism and the Intellectuals*